The Era of YIPS

By Luis Daniel Cortes

Disclaimer: The opinions presented herein are solely those of the author except where specifically noted. Nothing in the book should be construed as investment advice or guidance, as it is not intended as investment advice or guidance, nor is it offered as such. Nothing in the book should be construed as recommendation to buy or sell any financial or physical asset. It is solely the opinion of the writer, who is not an investment professional. The strategies presented in the book may be unsuitable for you, and you should consult a professional where such consultation is appropriate. The publisher/author disclaims any implied warranty or applicability of the contents for any particular purpose. The publisher/author shall not be liable for any commercial or incidental damages of any kind or nature.

Copyright © 2014 Luis Daniel Cortes

All global rights reserved in all media

ISBN-13: 978-1503043183

ISBN-10: 1503043185

First edition published

November 2014

Dancortes.com

P.O.Box 32123

Philadelphia, Pennsylvania 19146

This book is dedicated to everyone who has had to fall on their face repeatedly for lack of proper guidance and mentorship in the process of seeking a livelihood.

Table of Contents

INTRODUCTION

SECTION ONE: THE MACRO-ECONOMIC VIEW

THE CHANGING ECONOMY – 3

WHY ECONOMICS SHOULD MATTER TO JOBSEEKERS – 9

THE FIVE DIFFERENT TYPES OF ECONOMIES – 13

CAPITAL MOVES AND CREATIVE DESTRUCTION – 20

FREE-MARKET CAPITALISM BREAKS DOWN BARRIERS, STATE-CARTEL CAPITALISM ERECTS THEM – 23

THE ESSENTIAL ROLE OF CAPITAL, CREDIT, PROPERTY RIGHTS AND RULE OF LAW – 26

COOPERATION, INNOVATION AND RISK MANAGEMENT – 27

WHAT YOU SHOULD TAKE AWAY FROM ALL THIS – 29

SECTION TWO: THE CHANGING NATURE OF WORK

HUMAN AND SOCIAL CAPITAL – 38

HUMAN CAPITAL AS THE MEANS OF PRODUCTION – 41

HUMAN CAPITAL IS DIFFERENT FROM FINANCIAL/MATERIAL CAPITAL – 44

MASTERY AS THE MEANS OF PRODUCTION – 46

CREATING VALUE AND THE WORK SPECTRUM – 49

THE PREMIUM OF LABOR – 51

CREATING VALUE WITH HUMAN AND SOCIAL CAPITAL – 57

ALIENATION AND WORK – 59

SECTION THREE: THE CORE SKILLS AND VALUES THAT CREATE ECONOMIC VALUE

VALUES AS THE INCUBATOR OF ECONOMIC VALUE – 66

INVESTING IN OURSELVES – 70

WORKING KNOWLEDGE OF FINANCIAL RECORDS AND PROJECT MANAGEMENT – 72

SECTION FOUR: HIGHER EDUCATION HAS FAILED STUDENTS AND THE ECONOMY

THE OLD SYSTEM: SCARCITY OF MEDIA AND KNOWLEDGE – 81

WORLD WAR II AND THE ADVENT OF THE FACTORY MODEL – 82

THE HIGHER EDUCATION CARTEL – 83

CHARGING A PREMIUM FOR ELITIST SOCIAL CONNECTIONS: THE SPOILS SYSTEM – 86

THE ECONOMY CHANGED; THE FACTORY MODEL DIDN'T – 87

DEGREE INFLATION AND THE FALSE PROMISE OF SPECIALIZATION – 89

A CREDENTIAL/DEGREE DOES NOT VERIFY MASTERY – 93

THE ACCREDIT YOURSELF MODEL – 96

NOT JUST CHEAPER, BUT BETTER – 98

SHOULD I GET A COLLEGE DEGREE? – 99

SUMMARY: PUTTING THE ACCREDITING YOURSELF MODEL TO WORK FOR YOU – 103

SECTION FIVE: ACCREDITING YOURSELF

- THE NEED TO ACCREDIT YOURSELF – 104
- THE NECESSARY STEPS TO ACCREDIT YOURSELF – 105
- THE PROCESS OF PROFESSIONALISM – 109
- SELF-AWARENESS/SELF-KNOWLEDGE AND SELF-MANAGEMENT/SELF-DISCIPLINE – 111
- CLARIFYING WHAT MONEY AND SUCCESS MEAN TO YOU – 113
- THE VALUE OF AUTHENTICITY IN AN INAUTHENTIC WORLD – 114
- THE DIFFERENCE BETWEEN FAMILIARITY AND MASTERY – 116
- SELF-LEARNING TO MASTERY – 118
- RESOURCES FOR THE STUDENT AS TEACHER – 121
- ENTREPRENEURIAL SKILLS – 123
- MAINTAINING MOTIVATION – 123
- JOINING NETWORKS OF COLLABORATION – 126
- ACTIVELY SEEK PROBLEMS TO SOLVE – 128
- DOCUMENTING AND SHARING YOUR COMPLETED PROJECTS – 133
- SOLICITING THIRD-PARTY VERIFICATION AND TESTIMONIALS – 135
- THE VALUE OF A PROFESSIONAL BLOG/WEBSITE – 136
- ACCREDITATION AND SELF-EMPLOYMENT – 137
- THE GOAL OF ACCREDITING YOURSELF: TO BE THE ONY ONE WHO DOES WHAT YOU DO – 137

SECTION SIX: PUTTING IT ALL TOGETHER

WHAT IS SECURITY? – 138

NEW MODELS OF OWNERSHIP, WORK AND COLLABORATION – 141

INTEGRATING THE MATRIX OF WORK – 142

MOVING TO AN INFRASTRUCTURE OF OPPORTUNITY – 143

MANAGING CHANGE – 143

BECOME THE PERSON EVERYONE WHO OWNS THE OUTPUT WANTS TO WORK WITH – 145

Introduction

This book is not your average career counseling book because everything I have ever published thus far I have done so out of necessity: the economy is changing and it now takes a much broader understanding to secure a livelihood.

In the conventional view, the job seeker needs to find out where his passions lie and then go pursue it through a college degree. Most career counseling books have exercises to help you learn about yourself so you can figure out what your career should be. After having read so many of those books I can say they were not very useful to me. The reason why I say this is because self-knowledge is only one-fourth of what's needed to secure a livelihood in today's economy. Today we must understand the emerging economy—the parts of the economy that are expanding and offering opportunity—and the changing nature of work. Lastly, we must understand the role of lifelong learning in the emerging economy.

Just learning about what your interests are is no longer enough; that's the equivalent of being tossed into a wilderness with no map, no compass, no GPS or supplies and being told to rely only on your interests and talents.

Jobseekers need to understand the economy and the world of work they're navigating; without that knowledge, they're flying blind and the odds are not in their favor.

This book is my attempt to assist others in tilting the odds in their favor, whether you are a high school or college student, a recent college graduate, someone pondering graduate school to advance their career, someone recently laid off from a job or someone re-entering the workforce after a long absence. In the title of my book you see the strange term YIPS, but what is a YIPS? The term YIPS stands for Your Interdisciplinary Problem Solver which is a person who utilizes a variety of disciplines as well as hard skills in specific fields and soft skills that enable ownership of tasks and projects, systematic application of creativity and critical thinking, and professional standards of collaboration and conduct.

We have to let go of the concept of job security, that doesn't exist anymore if it ever did and I know it's hard to get over it psychologically. The only thing that exists now is opportunity and we have to approach job search in that manner. There are no guarantees; all we can do is shift the odds in our favor through our own efforts and learn to recognize opportunity.

This book will give you some insight into the knowledge and tools you will need to shift the odds in your favor.

The most important college-level course that is not taught in the universities today will be covered in this book: establishing and managing a livelihood.

The deeper the hard skills and knowledge, the more difficult it is to acquire.

I will attempt to take you on a journey I have taken myself, as a student, job seeker, employee, supervisor, mentor, and beginner. I have studied the major dynamics in our economy and society in depth so I can offer you the practical knowledge you will need to tilt the odds in your favor, whatever field you enter and whatever your present situation.

The economy is undergoing a tumultuous transformation that will last our entire lives. We can bemoan what will be lost and demand that the present remain unchanged, but life does not stand still; it advances, evolves and adapts and so must we. We have a choice: we can cling to what is already lost and go down with the ship or we can advance and adapt and overcome.

Security comes not from a government guarantee but from embracing opportunity. Security is a scarce commodity that everyone is searching for, meanwhile opportunity is abundant and most people are afraid to search for it. It's our choice: we can compete with the herd crowding around the dwindling pool of supposedly secure jobs or we can escape those poor odds and learn how to recognize opportunity, solve new problems and create value.

Joining the increasingly restive herd jostling for a place at the pool's edge guarantees a scarcity of winners and an abundance of losers, an imbalance that insures unhappiness and frustration.

The odds favor those who look elsewhere for opportunity, and those with an ability to solve new problems and create value in a variety of circumstances. If that sounds good to you, then this book is for you.

Section One: The Macro-economic View

To tip the odds in our favor, we need to understand these three subjects:

1. The changing economy
2. The changing nature of work
3. The role of lifelong learning

Later sections will lay out a practical guide to putting this knowledge to work in getting a job, establishing a livelihood and building a career.

The Changing Economy

The economy is unstable for a number of structural reasons, and this instability is not going to go away any time soon. Though we have been taught that the economy cycles between growth and recession—what's known as the business cycle—the growth of the past decade has been uneven at best. Beneath the surface, the economy is changing in fundamental ways that are confounding policy-makers mired in conventional thinking.

Some parts of the economy are shrinking because they are obsolete and fatally inefficient. Other parts are expanding because they are far more efficient than what they're replacing. They are in effect two economies mixed together, and the first step for anyone seeking a livelihood is to realize that opportunities in the shrinking sectors will be considerably fewer than those in the expanding sectors.

As a result of technology, the nature of work is also changing rapidly. The shrinking sectors will still offer conventional jobs, but as technology leapfrogs the obsolete and inefficient, even these traditional jobs will be changing. Those who can't adapt to the new modes of work will be left behind.

In the conventional view, a college degree prepares one to enter the workforce. Although certain sectors such as nonprofits and certain investment firms with a wide retail clientele still believe that, it is actually no longer true, as higher education has failed to keep pace with technology and a fast-changing economy. Anyone seeking a livelihood must also understand the new role of education in the emerging economy.

In advanced economies such as ours, the costliest sectors are healthcare, education, government and national security/defense. Traditionally, these have long been considered stable sectors with guaranteed job security. Ironically, this is changing, as the soaring costs of these sectors now exceed the economy's ability to fund them.

If an economy expands by 2% each year and healthcare costs rise by 10%--there isn't enough income generated by the economy to fund its continued expansion.

In other words, the disruption of sectors with fast rising costs is guaranteed. What this means for jobseekers is the traditional sources of job security are precisely the sectors that will be disrupted the most as costs will bring down as a matter of necessity: either costs will be controlled or the nation slips into insolvency.

How does an inefficient agency or enterprise cut costs? Since the largest expense for the vast majority of organizations is labor, the only way to make a significant impact on costs is to shed employees.

Whether we like it or not, enterprises don't have profits, they only have expenses.

While government agencies don't have profits, government depends on the profitability of private enterprise for taxes. A business can only afford to pay employees if it is viable, that is, makes a profit. Companies that don't make a profit lose money and close their doors; unprofitable businesses vanish, along with their payroll and the taxes paid by the company and its employees.

Governments get around this dependence on profitable enterprises for tax revenues by borrowing money. The government borrows money by selling bonds: in exchange for a sum of cash, the government promises to return the buyer's cash at a later time with interest.

Borrowing money requires paying interest, which means that some portion of income is siphoned off to pay the annual interest. The more is borrowed, the larger the slice of your income that goes to pay interest on the debt. If your income doesn't grow faster than interest payments, eventually all your income goes to pay interest and you have nothing left to live on.

This is called insolvency, and the only way out of insolvency is to declare bankruptcy and wipe out all the debt you owe.

That debt is a liability to you, but it is an asset to the lender. The buyer of the bond gave the government cash for the bond. If the government defaults and doesn't return the cash, the bond owner's asset is wiped out.

That means the cash is no longer available to invest in something else. The default doesn't just harm the bond owner; it harms the economy because it reduces the capital available for productive investment.

This is important because anyone seeking a job or career has to understand that there is no free lunch in the long-term. Government, enterprises and households can borrow money to fund their expenses for a while, but eventually the interest catches up with them, and they go broke as the interest soaks up so much of their revenues that there's not enough left to pay essential bills.

Living off borrowed money is a fool's solution to rising costs. Eventually, income and expenses must align.

The point of this brief economic lesson is simple: the problems in our economy cannot be solved by financial trickery or by borrowing more money. Everyone, from individuals to households to companies to governments must eventually live within their means. The longer one lives beyond one's means with borrowed money, the more violent the re-alignment will be.

We have lived in an economy that depends on debt (borrowed money) and rising consumption for so long that we imagine this is always how it has been and how it will always be. Both assumptions are wrong. The shift away from debt-based consumption as the source of economic growth is inevitable, and this will have a profound impact on jobs and the nature of work.

In addition to these basic financial limits on debt and consumption, there are also limits imposed by demographics, resources and the environment. The workforce of most nations is ageing as people live longer and fewer children are born per family, placing greater financial burdens on the working age populace to fund the pensions and healthcare costs of a rapidly expanding elderly population. In response, people are working longer, but societies with costly pensions and healthcare systems are facing a widening gap between the numbers of people who are working full-time and paying taxes and those drawing retirement benefits.

Once the ratio of full-time workers to retirees drops to two workers to each retiree, it becomes financially impossible to fund the costs of retirement without taking most of the workers' wages as taxes. This sets up a politically irresolvable generational conflict.

In the U.S., we are already at that threshold: as of 2013 there were 57 million Social Security beneficiaries and only 114 million full-time workers.

Resources are being depleted and what is being extracted is rising in cost. Global fisheries, for example, are in a steep decline as the world's fishing fleets strip-mine the seas. Even those who maintain that there is still plenty of oil and natural gas concede that the cheap, easy-to-get oil has been consumed; it now takes extraordinarily expensive measures to discover and extract deep oil. Extracting, refining and shipping hydrocarbon fuels now require more energy. This means it now takes more capital (investment of money) and energy to extract the same number of barrels of oil than it did in the past.

The environment is also under pressure as billions of people in developing economies pursue a high-consumption middle-class lifestyle. Freshwater aquifers are being drained, imperiling the sustainability of agriculture and urban centers, and soil depletion and air quality have declined precipitously in many heavily populated regions.

For all these reasons, the assumption that rapidly rising debt and consumption are sustainable is false.

From the perspective of sustainable prosperity, growth based on debt-based consumption is the road to ruin, as the foundations of fast-rising debt and ever greater consumption are crumbling.

This shift from debt-based consumption to a more productive sustainability is bringing profound changes to the nature of work itself and social arrangements in the workplace.

Stagnation in opportunities to work and earn, that is, a financial recession, leads to social recession, a loss of opportunities for adulthood: a rewarding career, family, and a home of one's own. In a social recession, for the 13er generation, it's devastating and depressing and the unemployed young millennial generation may be mired in adolescent narcissism, eschewing ambitions not just in work but in romance and marriage.

In summary, the notion that progress requires higher levels of consumption, all funded by ever-rising levels of debt, has run aground on the reality of limited resources, the destructive consequences of ever-rising debt and the loss of certain jobs to automation, robotics and software.

From a macro-economic view, it's clear the current system of defining progress as ever-higher levels of debt and consumption is no longer viable for a number of structural reasons.

We need to redefine progress as something sustainable: an economy that prospers with little to no debt and declining levels of consumption. Ultimately, the emerging economy is all about doing more with less, and creating value and solving problems with fewer resources. That's where the opportunities are expanding, and that's where the work will be.

The idea that happiness and fulfillment required ever more consumption was always flawed; it was a marketing ploy to sell more goods and services, not an idea grounded in what we were taught growing up. The more we learn about happiness and fulfillment, the more apparent it becomes that family, community, meaningful work and network of colleagues, collaborators and friends are the sources of happiness and fulfillment, not the accumulation of stuff: more expensive homes, more shoes, etc., turn out to have little impact on happiness and fulfillment.

As a result, understanding the economy also means understanding the changing nature of work and value creation.

Let's start with a quick overview of economics and why it matters.

Why Economics Should Matter to Jobseekers

What does economics have to do with my getting a job and building a career? The short answer is: everything. You are going to review many magazines that show you what sectors are growing and which are not, but it does not necessarily clarify what choices to make for jobseekers. I am going to attempt to illustrate a more concrete set of examples of the importance of knowing how a changing economy affects us as jobseekers. Take for instance the automobile industry, prior to that it was the horse and buggy, so if you still delivered milk on that horse and buggy while your competitor used an automobile, you were using a dying technology and your business would have vanished to more efficient competitors as a result.

Another economic force is a central government known forthwith as *the State* and its mechanisms of control, globalization and monopolies/cartels. It is said that modern capitalism is a reaction to the inequality, lack of opportunity and stagnation of the feudal economy. Some argue that large corporations established monopolies that could set prices without regard to market forces in the early 20th century, but my reading of the economy in that era does not confirm that. My understanding is that monopolies were formed by large corporations due to their connection to government who made regulations allowing monopolies to corner the market. That still goes on today with car insurance, the dairy industry and now the Affordable Care Act allows a cartelization of the healthcare industry.

The point for those seeking a career is this: what's riding high at the moment may be poised to reverse, and what seems like an industry that's dead in the water may be about to resuscitate.

Here's another example I would like to illustrate. Back in the early 20th century, there were hundreds of local beer breweries. When the federal government imposed Prohibition in the 1920s, these were closed down. When Prohibition was repealed in 1933, alcohol was once again legal and breweries re-opened.

The competitive advantage of large companies became a dominant force in the U.S. economy starting in the war years of the 1940s, and a consolidation trend swept through the economy. Small local breweries were bought up by larger firms, and by the end of the 1970s, there were only a handful of corporate breweries in the U.S.

Anyone who wanted a career in a local micro-brewery was dead in the water: there were no micro-breweries at all. But this extreme concentration of ownership and the limited choices that resulted sparked a reaction: the micro-brewery industry has flourished since the 1980s, and now hundreds of local micro-breweries are creating thousands of jobs and reinvigorating towns and urban neighborhoods but not without the continued attempt of government trying to assist the cartels in maintaining market share while getting free money. For example, back in 2010 three bars in the city of Philadelphia were raided for the non-crime of selling beers that were not properly registered with the state.

For the past decade, healthcare has been expanding rapidly in the U.S., and virtually everyone believes that healthcare will continue to offer plentiful job opportunities as this expansion will certainly continue for decades to come as the population ages and the demands for more healthcare increase.

But healthcare is now so costly, absorbing almost 20% of the nation's GDP (Gross Domestic Product), that it is poised to reverse course as the need to cut costs become paramount. Since labor is the largest expense, one way to cut costs is to replace labor with software and reduce the need for high-cost labor through new processes.

Since 40% of total U.S. healthcare costs are estimated to be paper-pushing—insurance claims, reviews of claims, etc.—it's blindingly obvious that streamlining the payment process could save billions of dollars. Such a streamlining is necessary, and it will reduce the number of workers processing paper in the system.

An extraordinary percentage (as high as 40%) of Medicare expenses are fraudulent, needless or counterproductive. Clearly, the system is ripe for reforms that slash needless expenses (and jobs).

Higher education is another case in point. For decades, anyone with a PhD degree could count on a job somewhere in the college/university system, as the number of those with PhDs was small and the sector was expanding. Given that the number of PhDs was limited and the demand for instructors was rising, basic supply and demand made getting a PhD a low-risk career choice.

But all that has changed. As more people flock to the "sure thing" of earning a PhD, the number of those with advanced degrees soared. As the cost of college tuition has skyrocketed, there are no limits on the expansion of higher education. Technology is offering new methods of teaching and learning, and there is now a surplus of PhDs and master's degrees.

Soaring costs are causing a reaction that promises to slash costs and jobs in higher education. Add the surplus of qualified candidates and we have a much different supply-demand situation: no wonder so many PhDs are underemployed or unable to land a tenured spot in academia.

If we understand that the economy is an ecosystem that goes through life, death, transformation and rebirth, then we understand the importance of developing skills that can be transferred from one sector to another.

There will always be a need for nurses, dental hygienists, welders, carpenters, researchers, etc., but that doesn't mean there will automatically be jobs for everyone who is qualified to work in these fields. Supply and demand are constantly shifting, and the odds generally favor those who seek fields with a shortage of qualified applicants, or fields that are too new to have credentialing programs, where experience counts more than degrees.

Everyone seeking a livelihood has to be aware that the pace of these changes is speeding up: what looks secure now could be insecure in a few years down the road. Security comes not from betting on whatever is riding high at the moment but from developing skills that are valuable in all sectors.

Even traditional fields such as law enforcement, healthcare and government are being transformed.

Understanding basic economic concepts helps us realistically assess the job market and make strategic decisions that improve our odds of success. For example, it's been found that small companies that are expanding create the most new jobs; large corporations create few new jobs, and small businesses that stay small tend to lose almost as many jobs as they create as new small business jobs are offset by those that are lost when small businesses close down.

Joseph Schumpeter coined the phrase creative destruction as the process of capitalism and he was correct. We cannot blame capitalism for the instability in our economy and we cannot use socialism as a solution to the creative destruction. The creative destructiveness of capitalism in the form of new technologies and processes is like a genie that cannot be kept in the bottle. As I said before capitalism goes through life, death, transformation and rebirth. Every nation or industry that tries to protect itself from this either stagnates or fails.

In the next section I will share a brief economics lesson and I promise it will be painless and abridged.

The Five Different Types of Economies

Let's start with a quick overview of the five major economic theories that dominate our era.

If you have an interest in economics, these are already familiar. If not, you've probably seen the key words in media stores. The points I want you to take home in this overview are:

1. Systems decline once extremes are reached.
2. Systems have a lifecycle of expansion, maturity and decay.
3. All economic systems are reactions to the extremes of previous systems.

For example, modern free-market capitalism arose in reaction to the limits of the feudal system and Marxism arose to explain how unrestrained capitalism leads to the dominance of finance, uncompetitive monopolies and the impoverishment of labor.

The failure of free-market capitalism (a premise that is open to debate) to escape the Great Depression led to Keynesian policies of stimulus and deficit spending.

Government regulations on capital led to slow growth, which triggered the neoliberal capitalist agenda of loosening regulations to spur growth.

The inequalities (an economy of winners and losers) of unfettered capitalism led to state socialism, where the government reduces inequality by taxing those with high incomes and using the tax revenues to fund social programs for low-income and unemployed citizens.

In roughly the order of their emergence on the world stage, the following is the five different types of economies:

1. *Modern Capitalism*: this is the classical free-market capitalism: supply and demand discover price of goods, services, labor, money and risk in open, transparent markets. Business cycles are an expected feature of free-market capitalism; when credit expands, so does the economy; when credit contracts, marginal investments become insolvent and are written off; the result is recession.
2. *Marxism*: developed by Karl Marx in the second half of 19th century, Marxist analysis holds that private capital has a built-in advantage over labor, and left to its own devices capital will impoverish laborers and enrich the owners of capital. The most profitable state of affairs for capital is not competitive free markets but the elimination of competition with monopolies of cartels.

   There are multiple forms of capital (industrial, financial) but the dominant form is financial. Advanced capitalism boils down to the dominance of finance capital over industrial capital and labor. The impoverishment of labor leads to the crisis of capitalism, as eventually there aren't enough workers with sufficient income to buy the goods produced by capitalism. The Marxist critique drove the development of various flavors of socialism.
3. *Socialist State Capitalism*: unfettered capitalism creates great disparities in income and wealth (again an economy of winners and losers). The solution is to extract wealth from the free-market winners via taxes for social programs that distribute the nation's wealth more equitably. To keep private capital from dominating the economy and ruling the nation, the state owns or controls key industries.
4. *Neo-Keynesian State Capitalism*: to counter recessions, the state (government) increases its own borrowing and spending (called deficit spending) to compensate for declining private consumption, and the central bank lowers the cost of borrowing money and floods the banking system with credit to persuade households and businesses to borrow money to spend and invest.

5. *Neoliberal Global Capitalism*: government regulations and meddling (picking winners and losers rather than letting the free market select winners and losers) hampers growth, and without growth prosperity declines for rich and poor alike. The solution to cut regulatory red tape and unleash markets to allow the free flow of information, labor and capital. This freedom increases the pie of wealth for everyone in the economy.

It's important to note that these systems do not necessarily replace one another; in the modern post-World War II era, each new system is layered on top of the existing arrangement. Thus state socialism didn't replace free-market capitalism; it was added as a new layer that distributed income to social programs and controlled key industries. The increased role of the state (Keynesian policies) influenced free-market capitalism but did not displace it, and neoliberal globalization extended the free flow of capital even as it left many domestic industries virtually untouched.

A couple of the takeaways from this brief lesson are that:
a. None of these systems is transitioning to a sustainable economy with plentiful opportunities: all are outdated and structurally flawed.
b. Every major economy is a mix of two or more of these concepts.
c. All these systems share a central faith in centralization: increasing centralization is seen as the solution to all problems.
d. Large, centralized systems are the wrong unit size for today's problems.

Let's examine these four takeaways in greater depth.

Every system reaches saturation, and the expansion phase ends. We see this all the time in retail chains: some new franchise explodes on the scene, rapidly multiplies until it seems like there's one on every block. Eventually the market is saturated, no new stores open, and the next phase is the chain closing hundreds of underperforming stores.

In the case of college tuition and fees, these have reached the level where the majority of families cannot pay them without a loan that is as large as a home mortgage.

We continue to do things in the way they have worked in the past without facing the problems as new and unique and coming up with appropriate solutions. Our economy has the largest debt on the planet yet investment companies continue to tell their retail investors that bonds are a safe haven.

All these economic systems have reached diminishing returns; all are failing. Yet we cling to them because we're convinced that because they made sense in the past, they will continue to make sense in the present.

It's worth noting that four of the five economic systems are basically unchanged from the 19th century, and the fifth (Keynesian deficit spending) originated in the early 1930s. Consider how much has fundamentally changed since 1930, in demographics, technology, globalization, energy, resource depletion, etc., and then consider that all of these enormous transformations are supposed to be explained and managed by ideas that arose in a much different era.

We are hard-wired to keep using what has worked in the past, even when it is failing, and to blame this systemic failure on a lack of something outside our control (a limited budget, etc.).

The solution doesn't require new technologies as much as it requires a new way of organizing the economy. Yet the mainstream of education, government, media, think tanks, business, unions, etc., clings to these concepts that were devised in much different eras and circumstances. We substitute problems with solutions we already know for the real problems that need new solutions.

There are no 100% ideologically pure economies—virtually every major economy is a complex mix of free markets, social program spending, Keynesian stimulus and neoliberal globalization. The U.S., widely considered a free-market economy, devotes $2.5 trillion of its $3.8 trillion federal budget to social programs. European nations such as Germany that are considered social-democratic rely heavily on globalization and exports to fund their social spending. China, nominally communist, relies on free markets to generate the revenues needed to subsidize state-owned enterprises (SOEs).

The point I want you to take away from this is that we don't have socialist economy, we don't have a capitalist economy, but instead we have a multitude of economies mixed together. These economies co-exist, and can be imagined as layers that overlap each other in certain areas but operate by their own rules and inputs.

For example, those with jobs in state social programs are working in a quite different environment than those exposed to free market forces. Those working in globalized sectors have a much different set of conditions than those working in domestically protected sectors such as law enforcement.

Protected sectors such as law enforcement and state social programs are entering into diminishing returns, pressures to modernize and cut costs are inevitable.

It is essential to understand the economy's multiple layers, because each one operates on a different wavelength and requires a different set of career strategies.

Though free market economies allow for a wide spectrum of businesses, modern capitalism is dominated by cartel-state capitalism: most of the power, capital and control have been aggregated into centralized cartels and the government.

In most areas, there are only two providers of health insurance; there are often only one or two providers of broadband internet service; in every major city there is only one major public transit company. The same used to be true of mobile phone services, but that is changing now. Fast food is dominated by a handful of national chains, as are grocery stores.

Centralization has reached diminishing returns and is no longer yielding any benefit. Instead, it has become the problem, not the solution; what worked in the past no longer works now. Centralization as a solution has been leapfrogged by decentralizing technologies.

The World Wide Web enables decentralized networks of productivity and cooperation that operate without centralized authority. The most productive and lowest-cost system turns out to be decentralized, not a centralized arrangement where capital and political power are concentrated into the hands of a few at the top of the heap.

If solutions must be decentralized and distributed, then bureaucratic centralized organizations cannot possibly be a solution: they are the wrong unit size.

Since we are hardwired to grab a solution we know for every new problem rather than look for new solutions, it's to be expected that the vast majority of people are reaching for a solution they already know—one of these 19th century ideologies—rather than face the reality that these are no longer solutions, they are the problem.

How does this help everyone seeking a livelihood?

The systems that survive and prosper are those that are exposed to dynamics that force constant evolution, adaptation and innovation that is, coming up with new solutions rather than just grabbing an old one and hoping it solves the new problem.

Those people who are also evolving, adapting and experimenting with new solutions to new problems will always be in demand.

So the takeaway from this brief examination of various economies is this: seek sectors and organizations that are adapting and seeking real solutions, and try to become a person who does the same, regardless of what field you're working in.

Capitalism is thrown about as if it was one system, but free-market capitalism isn't monolithic: there are five basic types of capitalism, and once again those seeking a livelihood will push the odds in their favor by understanding that not all types of capitalism offer the same opportunities.

Broadly speaking, capitalism is an economic and social system based on private ownership and transparent markets for the exchange and distribution of goods and services. While these attributes of capitalism can be traced back to early trading communities, the modern version of capitalism depends on transparent markets not just for goods and services but also for capital, labor, risk and credit.

Transparent markets discover the price of goods, services, labor, capital, risk and credit, and as a result they provide discipline that discourages high-risk, low-return speculative bets, inefficiency and waste.

The core of capitalism is of course capital: capital that is invested to earn a profit, that is, accumulate more capital.

Capital is generally assumed to mean money, but non-financial capital is just as important as financial capital in a knowledge-based economy such as ours. This is why we will examine the five types of non-financial capital in depth later in this section.

Some attributes of capitalism can be viewed as expressions of human nature rather than ideological constructs. The pursuit of self-interest drives competition and what Adams Smith called the invisible hand of the market. It is also the reason that capital seeks the highest return.

Self-interest can easily veer into greed and avarice, and as a result all economic systems have the potential to exploit shared resources and other people. This is a feature not just of capitalism but of all social and political orders. The elites in feudal societies, monarchies, theocracies and socialist systems all manage the status quo to enrich themselves and preserve their power.

Capital Moves and Creative Destruction

When I was studying regional economic and social development at the University of Massachusetts in Lowell, a professor introduced me to a book called Capital Moves which was about the history of RCA moving from Camden, New Jersey to south of the border. The mobile nature of capital is one aspect of capitalism that disturbs many people—the idea that capital will flow to the highest return, regardless of national borders or religious, national and ideological loyalties.

Capital that doesn't seek to expand will fall victim to capitalism's process of natural selection known better by the phrase creative destruction: the only way innovation and productive investment can occur is if less productive investments and quasi-monopolies are dismantled.

Just like capital moves to obtain the highest return, the same can be said of mobile workers, who move in order to find better paying work or advance their career.

Just as financial capital must grow or face creative destruction, human capital—skills and knowledge—must also be constantly reworked to align with changing market and social forces. To decry this is to decry the reality that the world is constantly changing and we must adapt or suffer the consequences.

Traditional hunter-gatherer societies were engaged in a way of life that was inherently insecure. As a hunter, you have to constantly relocate to a new area looking for new sources of game. Traditional societies were thus geared toward conserving social systems that organized labor, authority, sources of food and water, etc. in ways that reduced such insecurity. A society's desire for security has favored traditional means of enforcing that stability while discouraging risk and innovation.

Capital enterprises are organized solely to seek profit and expand capital, and as a result they disrupt these established risk-averse social and economic arrangements. Since capitalism thrives on risk-taking, innovation, mobile capital and the free exchange of ideas, goods and services, it rewards disruptive improvements in productivity. As a result, capitalism soon outpaces traditional methods.

It is important to understand the democratizing power of modern capitalism's financial system. The core features of modern finance—joint stock companies, stock exchanges and risk-management hedges—were present in European hotbeds of capitalism by the 1400s. Capitalism's ability to raise capital from diverse sources and lend it to a variety of enterprises enabled a new class—entrepreneurs—to arise. From that point on, enterprise was not limited to the aristocracy; people outside the small circle of the feudal elite suddenly had access to capital.

Capitalism developed as a self-organizing way to share and price risk, and to spread losses from failed ventures and loans. By enabling small investors to pool capital, the system created a broad-based mechanism for distributing both profits and losses.

In a continuation of this dynamic, today the internet is enabling crowd sourced sources of credit such as micro-loans. Credit is escaping from the tyranny of the big banks and their partners, the central bank and state.

In our highly politicized society, it's become habit to render the world black or white, Left or Right, Conservative or Progressive, etc.: every trend is declared good or bad. Free-market capitalism (as opposed to the state-cartel version that dominates our economy) is neither good nor bad; it is simply a system that favors adaptation over conserving the traditional ways. Its innate drive to democratize capital is inherently progressive, and this is why state-cartel capitalism (also known as crony capitalism) seeks to eliminate competition and transparency, the two essentials of free-market capitalism.

What makes free-market capitalism easy to love or hate is that it disrupts social and economic arrangements without regard to borders, politics or our own likes and dislikes. Those who see it disrupting oppressive social and economic arrangements view it as liberating, while those whose security depended on inefficient, corrupt, obsolete systems maintaining power indefinitely view it as destructive.

Free-market capitalism is akin to natural selection in nature: it operates not on likes and dislikes or to protect those currently atop the heap but on what adaptations work best in a changing environment.

Free-Market Capitalism Breaks Down Barriers, State-Cartel Capitalism Erects Them

The core dynamic of capitalism in our era is the battle between free-market capitalism, which breaks down barriers that protect the status quo's profits, and state-cartel capitalism which erects barriers that keep out competitors and guarantee high costs and fat profits. Barriers protect the entrenched elites.

One example is print media's former lock hold on classified advertisements. Before craigslist and other free classified advertising websites, anyone wanting to sell something had to pay a newspaper to print a classified ad. The tiny ads were expensive, and classified ad income was a stable revenue foundation for newspapers.

The internet tore down that barrier, lowering costs to near-zero and destroying the classified-ad barrier.

In contrast, state-regulated cartels erect barriers that increase their profits by eliminating competition or raising the cost of doing business so high that no new enterprise can afford to enter the sector.

Another barrier is erected by enforcing artificial scarcity: now that education is digital, there is no technical reason why someone could not take college courses online, pass the exams online and be issued a diploma online, all for virtually free. The higher education cartel protects its vast income from college tuition by artificially restricting college diplomas.

Free-market capitalism tends to go around barriers with new technologies and social innovations. Free-market capitalism enables fast evolution and low-cost experimentation.

Peer-to-peer services such as AirBnB bypassed this capital intensive, highly regulated model of providing rooms to visitors by making any spare bedroom in a home or flat into an alternative hotel room. This system is opt-in, meaning anyone who wants to offer a room can do so, and anyone seeking a room can rent the room if they choose to do so. There is no centralized bureaucracy managing the options or choices.

The state-cartel economy is characterized by middlemen (distributors) that add layers of cost, while free-market capitalism seeks to cut out middlemen and enables sales directly from producers to end users. This is the basic strength of farmers' markets and farm-to-consumer networks.

Another example of state-cartelism is how the U.S. healthcare system erects barriers by withholding the price of services and obscuring the true costs of care, making it impossible for end users to make informed decisions based on competitive apples-to-apples comparisons of quality and price.

The state enforces barriers that protect cartels and professional guilds, always under the banner of protecting consumers. But beneath this public-service veneer, the agenda pushed by lobbyists is protecting status quo costs and profits.

Barriers are self-liquidating, meaning that the negative consequences of barriers—inefficiency, high costs, stagnation—eventually erode the barriers. At some point, people can no longer afford the high prices created by barriers, and a black market or informal economy arises to provide the goods and services which have become too expensive in the formal barrier-protected economy.

When middlemen and regulations add value, the value is noticeable to the end consumer. When they cease adding value and simply add cost (i.e. when barriers to competition have been erected), consumers abandon the protected sector and seek alternatives.

Free-market capitalism excels in developing alternatives that bypass or dismantle barriers, lowering costs, broadening choices, inviting competition and improving quality. State-cartel capitalism excels in erecting barriers to protect politically powerful guilds and cartels.

We can characterize the two as different approaches to security: state-cartel capitalism seeks security by suppressing competition and guaranteeing high prices and profits with centralized authority, while free-market capitalism seeks security and innovation, lower costs, transparency, voluntary choices and decentralized local control.

State-cartel capitalism seeks security with "too big to fail," while free-market capitalism seeks security with a concept of failing often enough and staying close to the needs of customers and local markets.

Which system is guaranteed to fail? The one that is too big to fail, as too big to fail means it is too big to be managed effectively in a centralized fashion.

Barriers enable people to get complacent. Those protected by barriers lose sight of the organization's purpose and ignore the symptoms as the organization slides into decline.

Which is better, creative destruction by superior methods, or the stagnation and high costs of protected cartels? In either case, the result is the same: barriers are self-liquidating.

The Essential Role of Capital, Credit, Property Rights and Rule of Law

Property rights, rule of law, capital and credit all have key roles in capitalism.

Capitalism is the force that raises the productivity of labor and creates the wealth of nations. Capital and credit-starved economies with limited private ownership rights are underdeveloped economies, as economist Hernando De Soto explained in his book, *The Mystery of Capital: Why Capitalism Triumphs in the West and Fails Everywhere Else*. In the chronically underdeveloped economies De Soto describes, households already possess the assets they need to make a success of capitalism. But they hold these resources in the form of houses built on land whose ownership rights are not adequately recorded, unincorporated businesses with undefined liability, industries located where financiers and investors cannot see them. As a result of the inadequate documentation of these assets, they cannot be readily turned into capital nor traded outside of narrow circles where people know and trust each other, cannot be used as collateral for a loan, and cannot be used as a share against an investment.

While in the West, capital is represented in a property document that can be used as collateral for credit, third world and former communist nations do not have this representational process.

Credit plays a key role in capitalism's success and also its failure. When credit is unavailable to entrepreneurs, innovations go begging and the economy stagnates. Conversely, when credit is so cheap and plentiful that unproductive projects are funded, the eventual collapse of these malinvestments brings down the entire financial system. (This is what happened in 2008.)

Attempting to build free-market capitalism without well-documented capital leads to political, social, and economic problems: glaring inequality, underground economies, pervasive mafias, political instability, capital flight and flagrant disregard for the law.

But this is not just a problem of former communist and Third World countries. The same was true of the United States in 1783 where squatters and small illegal entrepreneurs occupied lands they did not own. For the next one hundred years enforcing property rights created a quagmire of social unrest and antagonism throughout the young United States.

Cooperation, Innovation and Risk Management

One feature of capitalism that is rarely noted is the premium placed on cooperation. Subcontractors must cooperate to assemble a product, suppliers must cooperate to deliver the various components, distributors must cooperate to get the products to retail outlets, employees and managers must cooperate to reach the goals of the organization, and local governments and communities must cooperate with enterprises to maintain the local economy.

Innovative ideas, techniques and processes which are better and more productive than previous versions will spread quickly; those who refuse to adapt them will be overtaken by those who do. These new ideas, techniques and processes trigger changes in society and the economy that are often difficult to predict.

This creates a dilemma: we want more prosperity and wider opportunities for self-cultivation (personal fulfillment), yet we don't want our security and culture to be disrupted. But we cannot have it both ways. Those who attempt to preserve their power over the social order while reaping the gains of free markets find their power dissolving before their eyes as unintended consequences of technological and social innovations disrupt their mechanisms of control.

Yet rejecting free markets also fails to preserve the power structure, for a citizenry denied the opportunity to prosper chafes under a status quo that enriches elites and relegates the masses to stagnation and poverty.

The great irony of free-market capitalism is that the only way to establish an enduring security is to embrace innovation and adaptation, the very processes that generate short-term insecurity. Attempting to guarantee security leads to risk being distributed to others, or concentrated within the system itself. When the accumulated risk manifests, the system collapses.

The core dynamic of free markets is the causal links between the free movement of labor and capital, transparent markets, risk, adaptation and growth. Every attempt to eliminate risk, hinder the flow of capital, rig markets and limit disruptive adaptation leads to stagnation and eventual collapse as the inefficient, wasteful and corrupt elements of the economy absorb all the liquidity, starving the system of investment, innovation, accountability and initiative.

There are lessons here for jobseekers: playing it safe limits potential losses but it also limits potential gains. When an opportunity arises that requires higher risk, the risk sets up the possibility of big gains. We don't want to blindly take one big risk after another; that's a sure way to lose. The odds are best when the opportunity is low-risk and the potential gain is game-changing.

What You Should Take away From All This

The essence of non-exploitive capitalism is creative destruction of current systems as more productive/profitable ways become available and barriers protecting the status quo are torn down or bypassed. As a result, capitalism inevitably disrupts current economic and social arrangements.

The decades of stable employment that characterized the post-World War II era, long considered the birthright of every resident of advanced economies, were actually anomalies made possible by low-cost resources and rapidly expanding credit. Now that resources are no longer cheap and abundant, and credit has entered diminishing returns, the inherently disruptive nature of capitalism is transforming outmoded, obsolete, inefficient and diminishing-return systems and organizations.

We are entering an extended era of disruption comparable to the industrial revolution, an era in which stability comes not from working for one employer for 30 years but from owning skills, social capital and the means of production—terms we will explore in greater depth in following chapters.

In this era, security comes from embracing adaptation and learning, rather than trying to get hired by a centralized bureaucracy for life. This emerging era will favor YIPS that is

Your Interdisciplinary Problem Solver, where the more a person solves problems and creates value, the more influence they will have, as opposed to bureaucracies, which seek to eliminate individual risk and accountability.

As individuals, we must adapt to this era by accepting that security comes not from clinging to obsolete arrangements that are no longer sustainable but by becoming adaptable ourselves. Capitalism as well as Mother Nature favors those who are most adaptable, and the opportunities will be greatest in those sectors that are most hidebound, where the gains to be reaped by transformation are the greatest.

Section Two: The Changing Nature of Work

It's not just the types of work that are changing—the nature of work itself is changing, too. The relationship between capital and labor, divided by a sharp line in the 19th century, has become much more complex in a knowledge-based economy—an economy whose growth depends largely on knowledge and the collaborative exchange of information.

In the industrial age of the 19th and 20th centuries, capital referred to large holdings of productive land (for example, plantations), large sums of cash that could be used to buy assets, or ownership of capital-intensive assets such as factories, mines, pipelines, electrical generation plants, etc. Assets that generate products or services are known as the means of production.

Ownership of large-scale capital and means of production were reserved for financiers, industrialists and the state.

Labor had one commodity to trade and sell: time. Since labor on farms, factory floors, etc., was largely interchangeable—there was little specialization and only limited roles for expertise—labor was itself a commodity much like the grain or manufactured items the workers produced. One hour of labor bought from laborer A was little different from the hour of labor bought from laborer B.

They key is the process of commoditization: when goods or services can be traded interchangeably in large quantities within free markets, these are commodities, as opposed to one-of-a-kind goods and services unique to one small-scale producer.

To a factory owner in 1910, the differences in skills within a group of 100 laborers made little difference (with the exception of highly skilled craftsmen such as tool and die makers): the assembly line moved at the same rate regardless of which individuals were on a particular shift.

Even skilled labor can be commoditized: selling life insurance to the masses requires a defined expertise in salesmanship from a licensed agent, yet Colonial Penn has been able to create their own sales pitches, license their employees and positioned them to pitch life insurance products on the phone to customers all day in such a way that makes these workers interchangeable.

Anything that is produced in bulk and that is interchangeable is a commodity. Though variations exist in commodities, they are still interchangeable and readily traded in markets.

What cannot be commoditized? A home-cooked family meal cannot be commoditized. A meal can be packaged in a factory and shipped to a market where the family can buy the meal, but this is not the same as a home-cooked family meal. Preparing and sharing a home-cooked meal is a shared, communal process; microwaving a package is not. The two are not interchangeable.

Money is a commodity and is interchangeable (so is credit).

One-of-a-kind objects that cannot be produced in bulk are not interchangeable and are not commodities. Examples include fine art (hence the value of passing forgeries off as the real thing), rare gemstones and items of historical significance. Goods that cannot be commoditized command high prices precisely because they are not being made in quantity and are not interchangeable.

Individuals with unique sets of difficult-to-define skills are not open to commoditization because they are not interchangeable and cannot be produced or trained in great numbers. For example, a biotechnology company may have a new treatment for a brain disorder that it wanted patented. The ideal candidate would be an M.D. trained in brain science who was also a patent attorney. These two disciplines could be divided, but to some degree the person writing the patent would be hobbled by a lack of deep understanding of brain science. While there may be a small number of qualified candidates, there will not be many due to the many years of training required to master two quite different specialties.

Another example is a company that manufactures specialty metal assemblies that uses welding robots to fabricate large orders of interchangeable parts. The company lands a contract for assemblies that cannot be reduced to a set of series of welds; a human welder can do many but not all the welds faster and cheaper than the robot, which must be reprogrammed. The ideal candidate for the job would be both an experienced welder and an experienced operator of the welding robot. This worker is not interchangeable with a welder or a robot operator.

Note the difference between the commodity labor and labor that is not interchangeable. What cannot be commoditized will command a higher value.

One of the basic trends of free-market capitalism is that increased specialization leads to more prosperity for everyone in the economy. The specialized worker produces more than the worker with generalized skills, and this increased production eventually lowers the cost of the product as the supply expands. The specialized worker makes more money because he produces more, and so it's a win-win: products decline in price even though everyone with specialized skills is earning more money.

But specialization does not necessarily mean the labor cannot be commoditized. Since any work whose processed and point of completion can be specified can be traded or automated, specialized tasks that are process-based work can still be commoditized.

Specialization is only a defense against work being automated or offshored if it is not process-based work and cannot be commoditized.

The only type of work that cannot be commoditized is work involving processes that cannot be specified in advance and whose point of completion is unknown.

Creative work is one example. It's difficult to specify each step of an advertising campaign, for example, because the campaign is a dynamic process that is changing constantly in response to what seems to be working and what new ideas come to the team. Even the point of completion is difficult to specify: what makes the campaign a success?

This is an interesting dilemma because there are skills in the private sector that today can be commoditized and therefore becomes a low-paying job such as life insurance sales. For example, Colonial Penn was able to take the task of selling life insurance and broke it down into simple-to-learn steps, it was commoditized and performed by anyone in the world who can speak, read and write English.

If you can commodify work then you can globalize it as well and globalization is not a recent phenomenon but a practice that goes back hundreds of years with trade in silk and other precious goods which may even go back thousands of years. Think about sugar, tobacco and tea that were enormously profitable commodities being shipped in great quantities thousands of miles by sea.

Advances in telecommunications and the internet have expanded global trade from goods to services: technical support calls, for example, can be handled by someone in a distant country.

Work that can be outsourced to employees overseas is a tradable service. Work that cannot be traded includes services that are localized, for example, repairing a porch railing.

Process-based work is generally tradable because the labor is commoditized; the people who complete the task are interchangeable. Work that cannot be specified is less tradable because the people who perform the work are not interchangeable.

In the previous era of globalization, the goods being traded were produced elsewhere because they could not be produced in the home market. Sugar cane, for example, does not grow well in England, so sugar was produced elsewhere and shipped to England.

What differentiates the present era of globalization is the trading of services such as tech support and software programming. This means that workers are competing with everyone else in the global village for work that is tradable. In this networked world, specialization is no longer a competitive advantage; the competitive advantage goes to those whose work cannot be commoditized or traded.

What is driving the commoditization of labor? The same force that drives the commoditization of goods and services: competition. Now that many services are also tradable, the marketplace for these services is global.

Since most of the workforce in advanced economies is employed in the service sector (as opposed to agriculture, mining, energy, construction and manufacturing), the commoditization and tradability of service labor is having an enormous impact on the delivery of services and on service labor.

It's important to understand that labor is the primary cost in the service sectors. As robots have replaced humans on factory assembly lines, the labor component of manufactured goods has declined. If you want to reduce the cost of a manufactured item, reduce the number of parts by 50% and/or the amount of material by 50%, you reduce the labor by 50%.

It's also important to note that the overhead costs of labor have risen dramatically in the past 20 years, and this trend shows no sign of reversing. The total cost of an employee is not just the wage/salary compensation; it includes all the labor-related overhead expenses: workers compensation insurance, disability insurance, the employer's share of Social Security and Medicare taxes, unemployment insurance, pension contributions, vacation pay and healthcare (assuming employer pays some or all of the employee's healthcare insurance costs).

Depending on the locale, industry and the age of the employee, these overhead expenses can nearly equal the wage/salary. In other words, if the employee's wage is $2,000 a month, the total compensation costs to the employer might be $4,000 a month.

Given the steady rise in healthcare and other overhead expenses, the employee may be wondering why he hasn't received a raise in years, while the employer is looking at the rising costs of benefits and total compensation costs. The employee might be costing the employer an additional $500 a month but all of this money is invisible to the employee, as it goes not to him but to healthcare insurance premiums.

This is why it's necessary for the nation to lower the costs of state-cartel systems like healthcare; as these price-insensitive, politically protected systems continue to increase their share of the national income, there's less money available for wages outside the cartel.

In other words, the pressure on wages has little to do with any one employer or sector; it results from systemic distortions in the economy and global competition that cannot be put back in the bottle.

Machines have a built-in cost advantage over human employees, simply because they do not incur labor overhead costs: they do not get sick, do not need vacations, do not go on strike, and their costs of maintenance are more predictable than the costs of healthcare for human employees.

All these factors push employers to reduce labor costs by commoditizing work so it can be automated or performed by cheaper labor overseas.

Though much work has been commoditized, and much more can be commoditized, a significant amount of work cannot be automated or performed overseas; this includes everything from lining domestic oil wells to understanding local markets.

For jobseekers, the key to take away from this discussion is this: those who don't understand the changing nature of work will likely stumble into career cul-de-sacs and blind alleys, seeking work that has already been commoditized or will shortly be commoditized, at a loss as to why they can't find a job.

Once again: your advantage is knowledge.

What we need to understand is how both capital and labor have changed from the industrial era.

In a knowledge-based economy, capital isn't just cash or land or large-scale industrial plants. There are five types of non-financial capital that are as essential as financial capital in a knowledge-based economy. Two of these types of capital, human and social capital, are acquired by individuals through their own effort.

In the old industrial model, labor was a time-based commodity: laborers were paid for the time they spent toiling. While many low-skill jobs still pay by the hour, the hourly model no longer explains how work is valued. Higher-wage labor is not paid to perform processes that can be specified and automated or offshored; Higher-wage labor is paid to create value and solve problems, and so we need to understand these two processes if we want to establish a career with higher earnings.

While knowledge and skills are obviously critical in a knowledge-based economy, knowledge is not the only factor in creating value and solving problems. We need to understand the five types of non-financial capital: human, social, cultural, symbolic and infrastructural, and work that cannot be commoditized.

These five types of capital will form a part of what will give you the competitive edge as YIPS, Your Interdisciplinary Problems Solver.

These sections may require dedicated study, but it will be worth the effort: your advantage is knowledge.

Human and Social Capital

Human capital is an inexact term for labor's ability to take financial (money) and physical capital (tools) and create economic value.

Social capital is the value derived from connections to others: the sum of friends, alliances, memberships and networks that create reciprocal sources of value. The key word here is reciprocal, as social capital is a two-way dynamic: it's created by providing value to others, as well as deriving value from your association with them. Reciprocity is the heart of social capital.

One way to give the terms more precision is to consider the example of building a house: imagine that all the necessary tools and materials are laid out on the building site ready for you to go to work, there is a bank account with sufficient money to fund the construction, but you have zero building experience. Clearly, you will be unable to build the house because you lack the necessary hard skills of the building trades. You do not have the human capital needed to construct the house and created economic value out of the financial and material capital.

Without human capital, the financial and material capital is dead money. It is incapable of generating value, profit or wealth.

Suppose that you utilize your soft skills to organize others to build the house. The eight essential skills listed in the next section are the core soft skills of professionalism: being able to communicate effectively, take responsibility, be accountable, etc.

If you lack hard skills in building but you have an abundant set of soft skills, you will be able to recruit and manage others to build the house.

This illustrates why these eight skill sets are essential: they enable anyone who owns these skills as part of their human capital to create economic value, even if they lack the applicable hard skills at the start of the project.

It is vital that we understand that these soft skills are the foundation for hard skills: if one has the eight essential soft skills, one can learn hard skills. However, note that this does not work in reverse: having hard skills does not necessarily give a person the means to acquire soft skills.

To understand social capital, let's imagine two scenarios.

1. In the first case, the person tasked with building the house is given the site, cash and building materials in an unfamiliar locale where he is a complete stranger.
2. In the second scenario, the inexperienced builder is given the task in his home community, where he has friends, contacts and networks. Even if he doesn't know a single tradesperson or subcontractor, he can quickly utilize his social capital to identify trustworthy craftspeople to help him build the house.

    This is like arriving in a strange city but knowing a few well-connected people: suddenly the challenges of finding a place to live, a job, some friends, etc. all become immeasurably easier.

One key aspect of human capital is overlooked in conventional descriptions of the term, which focus on knowledge and skills. But human capital isn't just skills: it's having integrity and professional standards, being trustworthy, accountable and honest. It's practicing a set of values that create economic value.

I will illustrate the importance of these elements of human capital with an example.

Let's take two people with equal levels of skill, knowledge and experience. One is a manager in a corporate or government office and the other is part of an informal alliance of free-lance professionals who work together on projects. The office is of course hierarchical and the free-lance projects are opt-in—there is no boss to give orders, every participant is equal, though each project has one key sponsor who manages the contributions of the other free-lancers.

Examples of independent free-lancers include subcontractors in the construction industry, video and audio professionals within the film industry, and writers and graphic designers in new media.

Now let's say the corporate/government manager lacks integrity and professionalism; he goes back on his word, misrepresents the views of others to benefit himself, lashes out at subordinates when he is in a foul mood, plays favorites within the office, takes credit for the work of others, misrepresents his accomplishments and cons higher management into believing he is an effective manager.

If this person were in an opt-in free-lance work environment, how many other professionals would choose to work with him? Who would willingly subject himself/herself to such a toxic sociopath who would damage the livelihoods of anyone who worked with them? One experience would be enough and the word would quickly spread: avoid this person at all costs, not because they have no skills but because they have no integrity and no professional values.

This example also highlights the downside of bureaucracies and hierarchies: bureaucratic organizations by their very nature protect the venal and the incompetent because the purpose of a bureaucracy is to diffuse accountability so that no one person is ever responsible for the organization's failure except when it's convenient to blame the person who is lowest on the totem pole.

Human capital can only be fully valued in environments which value all aspects of human capital, not just a specific set of skills.

Human Capital as the Means of Production

The means of production are the equipment, money and expertise needed to generate goods, services and profits. In our earlier industrial economy, these were typically factories, mines, railroads, etc., assets that require a vast amount of financial capital and human labor to operate.

In the post-industrial economy, the means of production has shifted emphasis from financial capital (money) to knowledge. As the cost of the tools of production—robots and digital processing—decline, the means of production are increasingly knowledge-based.

Though post-industrial economies still need capital investment, the share of labor devoted to capital-intensive infrastructure (the electrical grid, railways, shipbuilding, etc.) declines as a percentage of total employment and economic output (gross domestic product, GDP).

Just as the percentage of the nation's capital and labor devoted to agriculture has declined precipitously (a mere 2% of the labor force now works in agriculture, down from 50% in the 19th century), so too has the percentage of the nation's workforce and capital needed to produce steel, autos, etc.

Those parts of the economy that leverage knowledge and relatively modest capital—digital media, software, 3D fabrication technology and programmable robots—have expanded their share of the economy. The more productive the sector, the more profits it generates, and this attracts more capital and talent.

The cost of the tools needed to produce high-profit goods and services is declining sharply. As a result, processes that once required costly machines and large factory spaces can increasingly be done by inexpensive desktop digital fabrication tools (namely, 3-D printers) that cost a few thousand dollars rather than millions of dollars.

Information technologies (IT) that once required a large staff have been automated to the point where a sole proprietor can produce output on a single inexpensive computer.

In other words, the means of production in the industrial age were extremely costly factories operated by thousands of low-skilled workers. The skills, talents, experience, goals and motivation of those individual workers—their human capital—had minimal impact on the overall output of the factory (with the exception of the tool-and-die workers who made the tools).

The human capital of assembly line workers was not worth much because the work was not sensitive to skill level of the worker: a completely inexperienced worker could acquire the necessary skills in a short time. In economic terms, the worker could not charge much of a premium for his labor because his human capital had little leverage in the production of goods, services and profits. On an assembly line, a higher-skilled worker doesn't produce much more than a lower-skilled worker.

The low-skill industrial worker didn't own the means of production—his economic value was limited to his time and ability to perform repetitive tasks.

Conversely, in a knowledge-based economy, the cost of human capital dwarfs the cost of machinery and tools. A desktop digital fabrication machine might cost a few thousand dollars, and the computer that runs the design software a few hundred dollars. Training the operator costs more than the tools. This is readily apparent in local government budgets, approximately 80% of which are devoted to labor costs. Though a city owns a large capital infrastructure of roads, vehicles, etc., the cost of this physical capital is considerably less than the human capital needed to operate it.

A networked economy offers new models of organizing work. An example is the open collaboration model of assembling human and social capital to complete a complex project with relatively little hierarchy and management. In this model, workers collaborate to complete a project and then move on to other work.

The financial equivalent is crowd-funding. In a traditional economy, anyone wanting to raise money for a new enterprise had to apply for a loan from a bank or an investment from a venture-capital fund. In the crowd-funding model, funds are raised from individuals.

The premium charged for the costly overhead of a bank or venture-capital fund vanishes; the costs of raising money have been reduced to low-cost server space and software.

Put another way, the premiums companies charge for financial capital and hierarchical structures of production are declining. The premiums earned by the classic advantages of corporations—access to financial capital and hierarchical management—are being eroded by new networked, collaborative structures of finance and production.

What I want you to take away from this discussion on the means of production is this: the emerging economy is accelerating the value of human capital in both financial and goods-and-services producing sectors.

Human Capital Is Different from Financial/Material Capital

There are critical differences between human capital and financial/material capital.

1. Human capital is inherently flexible and adaptable. Indeed, one of the key attributes of human capital is that we can learn new skills and apply these to new

fields. Human capital isn't just the sum total of a person's skills and knowledge—it is the ability to learn, adapt and experiment.

People who are willing to learn can keep ahead of the commoditization of labor by learning what cannot be commoditized or by moving their skills to a new field, in effect keeping ahead of commoditization.

If complexity is rewarded, we build human capital by adapting to complex workplaces. If simplicity is rewarded, we build human capital by learning how to break complexity down into simpler processes and fewer interactions.

2. All it takes to increase human capital is time, effort and experience. Given the abundance of lessons and resources on the internet, it requires little to no money to learn new skills other than the cost of the internet connection.

   Compare this to the arduous process of saving enough money (financial capital) to buy land or capital equipment.

   While we may not be able to accumulate enough financial capital to buy costly fixed-asset means of production, flexibility and adaptability are key components of our human capital—and these are free to develop.

3. Human capital becomes economically valuable when it creates value and solves problems. This requires mastery of a field, a topic we will explore later in this section. Mastery is cumulative; the more we know, the easier it is to learn more. Insights arise when expertise is applied to a new field—a process of

cross-fertilization that can be called multi-disciplinary or inter-disciplinary.

Mastery and multi-disciplinary or inter-disciplinary skills are generally resistant to being specified into processes that can be automated or commoditized, because mastery is an accumulation of experiences that develops into a highly effective but difficult to replicate intuition. Those who have developed mastery are able to see subtleties lost on the less experienced, and can refer to a vast database of similar situations for insight into solving a particular problem.

Those with inter-disciplinary and multi-disciplinary skills can apply insights from one field to another field in a process that is resistant to automation. Indeed, the point of completion—a better, cheaper, faster, more efficient way to get the same results—cannot even be specified, for the solution is not yet known.

Mastery as the Means of Production

Familiarity with a field is rarely enough to create value and solve problems. Familiarity may be enough for low-skill commodity labor, but knowing how to create value and solve problems requires mastery, for only mastery generates a premium. In the context of the previous section, we can define mastery as owning the means of production in a knowledge economy, for mastery is a key component of human capital. All the other components of human capital—flexibility, adaptability, self-discipline, learning how to learn, etc.—serve the goal of attaining economically valuable mastery.

Consider the case of an experienced handyperson who can troubleshoot and repair dozens of different problems in dwellings. The hand tools needed to perform the majority of these repairs are mass-produced and relatively inexpensive. The financial and material capital needed to create value as a handyperson is modest; the largest capital expense is transport to various jobs.

By themselves, these tools cannot possibly create any economic value; they are useless. In the hands of an inexperienced, low-skill worker, they will more likely be a force of value destruction rather than value creation. Only in the hands of an experienced, skilled knowledge worker can the tools create value.

The apprentice handyperson will lack the experience and skills to quickly and correctly assess the problem and determine the lowest-cost, most efficient means to repair the problem. The less skilled worker may well take five times as long to make the repair as the worker who has mastered all the required trades, and may well select repair options that cost more and are less effective.

In other words, mastery—deep expertise based on experience and ownership of the work—is the key element to value creation. Mastery is what creates a premium for human capital.

Mastery is not just a mix of knowledge, expertise and experience: it also requires ownership of the work, meaning that the master performs all work as if he owns every aspect of it: the process, the final product and the reputation that arises from the work.

The worker does not own their work, is careless and slipshod. The worker who owns knowledge and expertise but is incapable of owning their work can never achieve mastery.

It is vital that we understand that mastery is not just a collection of hard skills; it is also a value system of ownership of all work, no matter how menial it may appear to the outsider. In a very real sense, the worker who doesn't own his work does not really own the means of production.

To illustrate the mindset of mastery, let's consider garden maintenance as an example. The master gardener treats each of the yards in his care as if he owned it, and as if every aspect of his care is a reflection of his reputation and skill. It doesn't matter if the gardener's owner is rich or poor or pleasant or unpleasant; the work is done equally well for all because the master gardener owns all his work equally.

To establish and maintain a livelihood in the emerging economy, students must be able to build economically valuable mastery in their chosen field. Simply acquiring generalized knowledge will not be enough to create value.

In traditional economies, mastery is gained by serving a long unpaid apprenticeship with a master craftsperson. The master often owns his/her own workshop, and provides the apprentices with room and board. In exchange for years of hard labor, the master teaches the apprentices the processes and skills of the craft. Such apprentice-master craftsperson arrangements still exist in the traditional handcrafts of Japan.

Creating Value and the Work Spectrum

I have repeatedly described higher-value work as work that creates value and solves problems. To help differentiate between lower-value work that completes tasks and higher value work, let's look at various measures.

We can think of each measure as a work spectrum or sliding scale: the lower the work is on the scale, the less value it creates. The higher the work is on the spectrum, the more value it creates. When we overlay these measures we have an insightful way to measure the value of work.

We've already covered the first measure: how much of the work is process-based? As we've seen, the point of completion and each step of the way can be specified in process-based work, and this makes it programmable and tradable: process-based work can be automated or offshored, that is, commoditized.

Non-process-based work cannot be specified because the solution is not yet known.

Another measure is if the value is derived from empathy, compassion, touch and emotional support. This work is intrinsically non-programmable because the value is not created by a process but by a human connection. Though offshore workers can interact with each other via videoconferencing, and a robot can be programmed to mimic a human smile, digital and machine facsimiles of empathy are not interchangeable with authentic human empathy and caring.

Since the core attribute of commoditization is interchangeability, work that derives its value from human connections cannot be commoditized. I would caution that this type of work is not necessarily in high demand nor is there a scarcity of it and most of it is in the field of psychology which has become a platform for pushing pharmaceutical products.

In this spectrum of work we can arrange it from high-touch to low-touch interactions. For example, low-touch would be shopping online, where the processes and interactions are automated. Examples of high-touch include medical care, mentoring, sales and psychotherapy.

There is examples of high touch, low-skill work such as assisted living aide, while other high touch work require high-skill and experience such as a psychiatrist. The value isn't created by skill level but by the ability to give someone your full attention and form an emotional bond of empathy, compassion and respect.

The characteristics of work that is difficult to automate are mastery of skills that cannot be specified into repeatable processes, flexibility and high touch. These skills—along with the eight essential skills—are key characteristics of human and social capital.

Why does this matter to jobseekers? Let's take the example of someone learning to install glass. The beginner is not very productive, while the worker with six months experience is very productive. The worker with six years' experience is not much faster than the one with six months' experience, though he will likely know more about custom situations than the worker with six months experience.

The problem for the worker is that the value he can create (and therefore his wage) hits the top of the S-Curve in six months; he is already at or near his maximum earning power. Accumulating more experience won't increase his earnings unless he learns an additional trade or learns to manage a crew, that is, acquires new fields of knowledge that will increase the value of his skills/human capital.

To understand the S-Curve of value creation and earnings potential, we need to explore the concept of premium, that is, how work creates value.

The Premium of Labor

Let's start with three fundamental components of the economy:

1. The free market
2. The state (government)
3. The community, that is, all the activity and assets that are not priced by the market or controlled by the state. Examples include churches, neighborhood groups and non-profit organizations. These interact with both the market and state, but the purpose of the organization is not to reap a profit or enforce regulations and laws.

In the free market economy, revenues must exceed expenses, that is, the enterprise must generate a profit. Costs include:

- Materials,
- Labor and overhead (labor overhead includes employer's tax payments, unemployment

insurance, etc., while general overhead includes office rent, accounting, etc.),
- Capital investment (replacing or upgrading equipment and software)

If the enterprise loses money, it will eventually close, or bankrupt whatever entity is subsidizing the losses.

The current global economy is characterized by overcapacity: the supply of goods and services is larger than the demand. There are too many steel mills, hotel rooms, factories making TVs, etc., and relatively few manufactured goods that are scarce. This forces enterprises to reduce their input costs—the costs of production—to reap a profit.

In many cases, labor is the most expensive component of production costs. Labor must generate a premium, a gain in value beyond the cost of the labor. For example, if a company pays an employee an annual salary of $40,000, the firm must also pay labor overhead and benefits, costs which may add 50% to the base wage.

The company must also generate a gross profit large enough to fund capital investment, general overhead and a return on the capital invested in the enterprise.

Thus a worker paid $40,000 must generate $100,000 of economic value to justify his employment.

Since a robot and its digital software do not need healthcare, unemployment and disability insurance or a pension plan, the robot costs 50% less than the human worker even if the robot's operational costs equals the base wage paid to the human worker.

As the costs of digital technology fall and the ability of this technology to replace human labor increases, the premium generated by labor declines: if a robot that costs $20,000 a year to operate can replace a human worker being paid $40,000, the value of the human labor falls to the robot's operational costs, that is, $20,000 per year. Labor that cannot be replaced by software/machines or offshored generates a premium, especially if the labor is in a sector where prices are high due to scarcity of the good or service being produced.

Outside of cartels that fix the price of their products, the market dictates the scarcity/abundance and supply/demand for goods, services and labor. When there is an oversupply of goods, services and labor, the price of all three falls.

As the number of jobs that cannot be replaced by technology declines, the supply of labor increases. This supply and demand imbalance tends to drive wages down, as more workers compete for increasingly scarce jobs.

We need to distinguish between a premium and a subsidy. If the government pays above-market wages, it doesn't mean the state's labor force is creating a premium; it simply means the taxpayers are subsidizing the state workers' higher pay.

Let's take state-mandated labor at gasoline stations as an example. New Jersey is one of those states that require gasoline to be pumped by paid staff rather than by the customers. This is a policy decision that creates jobs that would not exist if customers pumped their own gasoline. The jobs are subsidized by buyers of gasoline (and perhaps taxpayers; the details vary from state to state).

There is a premium generated by someone pumping gasoline for customers, but the premium is only as large as what customers willingly pay extra for the service. If having gasoline pumped for you costs 10% more in the open market, then that is the premium that get subsidized.

Ultimately, all state subsidies are paid by the surplus generated by non-state workers and enterprises. That means there is a limit on how much the state can subsidize labor. The federal government could print unlimited sums of money, but eventually this will cripple the economy.

In the free market, labor can charge a premium if it is scarce (that is, few people have the necessary skills) or it creates high value in the marketplace. As noted earlier, mastery of skills that cannot be fully specified as repeatable processes, flexibility and high touch create economic value.

Conversely, if the skills are not scarce and/or the value created is low, the wages will also be low. This is why fast-food preparation is paid modest wages. The work is hard and fast-paced but doesn't require high skills, so the value created is relatively low. In a nation where the second largest spoken language is Spanish, modest wages are also paid to bilingual employees who serve in a customer service capacity. While knowing an additional language can be beneficial, the value created while in a customer service capacity is relatively low. How much premium are people willing to pay to be served fast food by a human worker? How much more of a premium is a customer willing to pay to have customer service representatives who speak their native language? We can ask the same question of retail purchases. Many people like being served by a human and will pay a premium for this service. Others would prefer to order online or be served by a machine if the cost is lower.

Being served fast food is low touch; there is little value in the human interaction. The workers are interchangeable, the definition of commoditized labor. In general, people won't pay premiums for low touch interactions, and so these processes are prone to being automated.

Since our fast-food meal is relatively similar to other fast-food meals, there is little premium placed on the skill of the preparer. Low touch, low skill work has little premium, so the benefits of automation are compelling to employers facing ever-higher labor overhead costs in an economy burdened with over-capacity.

In contrast, a restaurant can offer a high-touch, high-skill experience and thus it can charge a premium for its ambience, serve staff and freshly prepared meals. The labor generates the premium: a restaurant with an abundance of ambience will soon be deserted if the staff is incompetent and the food poorly prepared.

Some labor generates its value less from specialized skills and more from what Charles Hugh Smith calls high touch. These workers do not need lengthy skills-based training to create value; the value is created by high touch characteristics such as empathy and the professionalism embodied by the eight essential skills as outlined by Charles Hugh Smith. I am indebted to him for this understanding.

There are three sources of value creation. The higher the skill level, the larger the premium his/her labor can generate:

1. Process-based/non-process-based
2. Low-touch/high-touch
3. Experiential sensitivity, that is, the sensitivity of output to mastery

It's important to note that these sources of value do not necessarily align with the driver of higher earnings in the pre-software/robotics era: specialization. The key to higher earnings in the past was to specialize in one narrow field, as relatively few people would possess expertise in that specialty. The narrower the division of labor, the thinking went, the more productive the specialist and the higher the value of his labor.

But since specialized skills may well be more reducible to a process than generalized knowledge, specialization is not necessarily a panacea. There are other problems with specialization. One is that the narrower the field, the more vulnerable it is to changes in the market that render it obsolete.

Another is that the vast higher education industry has sought to market specialized advanced degrees as the solution to diploma inflation and the decreasing value of a college degree. One can now get a master's degree, for example, in casino management. Though this specialization promises some narrow expertise that might create a premium if there is a shortage of people with casino management experience, it becomes an albatross if no such demand exists: a specialized degree simply gives prospective employers a handy reason to reject the candidate as unqualified.

What I want you to take away from this section is that specialization no longer guarantees a premium for labor. Skills that are sensitive to mastery are difficult to specify and turn into a process, regardless of whether they are specialized or generalized. Specialization by itself does not confer resistance to commoditization.

What creates a premium in the emerging economy is professionalism, adaptability, skills that can be applied to new fields (that is, cross-pollination) and the ability to learn new skills.

Creating Value with Human and Social Capital

In this book I have stressed that the purpose of work is to create value and solve problems. In this section, we look at a small-scale example of how value is created in the emerging economy with social innovation.

Studies have found that human creativity is largely the result of sharing ideas and transferring innovations in one field to other fields. Innovation may arise from a single person, but its application requires human and social capital.

The two small-scale examples described below illustrate how human and social capital works in conjunction with community and financial capital.

Example: Neighborhood Bike Works in Philadelphia, PA, is an organization that started as a program of the Bicycle Coalition of the Delaware Valley and organized as a separate nonprofit in July 1999. They operate out of three locations throughout the city as well off-site programs where they partner with schools, recreation centers, and other community organizations. They offer classes in bicycle repair and free use of the shop's tools to do-it-yourselfers who want to repair their own bikes. It also provides bike repair services and sells used bicycles. The income generated by the repair service and sales of used bikes supports a small staff and enables the community free use of the shop's tools.

The amount of financial capital needed to start this enterprise was modest. The enterprise serves a wide spectrum of the community: students, do-it-yourselfers, those needing bike repairs or an inexpensive used bicycle. The classes aren't free and that opens the door for healthy competition. For example, there is another organization called Fairmount Bicycles that offer the ability for you to pay for one class at a time, so for those who would not be able to attend all four sessions or are only interested in a particular course, Fairmount Bicycles is a better option. They also offer to different class schedules.

These bicycle repair outfits did not require any technological innovation—it required social innovation. It illustrates that the profit motive—often held up as the only motivator within capitalism—is not the only motivation for either innovation or enterprise.

Human and social capital shows that creating value via social innovation does not necessarily require more financial capital—this can be summarized as doing more with less.

Value creation and problem-solving arise from many sources, not just the technological innovations that receive media coverage. If we combine the many sources of value creation unleashed by digital technologies, we realize that ours is one of the great transformative eras in human history.

Alienation and Work

In Marx's view, workers were alienated from the product of their work because they did not own the product or control the means of production. Marx argued that the absence of ownership and control was also an absence of agency (control of one's destiny) and meaning. Workers were estranged from the product of their work, from other workers and from themselves, as the natural order of the product of work belonging to the one who produced it was upended by capitalism.

Marx characterized this separation of work from ownership of the work and its output as social alienation from human nature. Capitalism, in his view, did not just reorder production into enterprises whose sole goal was profit and accumulating more capital; it destroyed the natural connection between the worker, the processes of work and the output or product of his work.

Marx was thus one of the first to analyze work not just in terms of economic output but in social and psychological terms.

The marketplaces' commoditization of everyday life—both parents working all day for corporations so they could afford corporate childcare, for example—

created two alienating dynamics: a narcissistic personality crippled by a fragile sense of self that sought solace in consumerist identifiers (wearing the right brands, etc.) and a therapeutic mindset that saw alienation not as the consequence of large-scale, centralized commoditization and financialization but as individual issues to be addressed with self-help and pop psychology.

So what do I want you to take away from this section as a job seeker? There are several things for you to take away from this section.

The first is that the source of value creation is linked to the level of agency (control of one's work) and ownership of the work: work that is not process-based (that is, that cannot be commoditized) and that is experientially sensitive to mastery enables a higher level of agency and ownership because the worker owns the means of production—his human and social capital.

The second is that the dramatic lowering of barriers to education and the ownership of tools powered by the internet has greatly expanded the opportunities to escape an alienating dependence on the state and cartels for employment and on superficial consumerism for meaning.

If we trust networks rather than states or corporations for our security, we automatically gain agency (control of our work and lives) and an authentic sense of self gained from owning our work and the results of our work.

It is important to understand that corporations exist to make a profit and accumulate capital, for if they do not make a profit and accumulate capital they will bleed capital and disappear. To believe that organizations dedicated to making a profit could magically organize society in ways that benefit every participant is nonsense. Corporations organize labor and capital to accumulate capital. It is absurd to expect that such organized self-interest magically optimizes the social order. This is not to blame all the ills of society on corporations; it is simply to note that corporations are limited by their limited purpose. Their purpose is not to organize a healthy, sustainable economy; it is to organize labor and capital in such a way that the corporation can accumulate capital in a marketplace controlled by supply and demand of the present.

Corporations have profited greatly from the alienation of work and the social order, as narcissistic debt-based consumerism is a highly profitable economic order, even if it is socially dysfunctional, unsustainable and destructive to individual agency and meaning.

We conclude this section on the changing nature of work by noting that the expansion of decentralized, distributed networks, the near-zero cost of knowledge and the declining cost of the means of production (digital memory and processors, software, 3-D fabrication machines, robots and tools) offer newfound opportunities for workers to reclaim their agency and ownership of their work and output.

Rather than rely on centralized states and corporations to organize labor and capital, collaborative networks can do so without alienating workers from their work and disrupting the sources of meaning.

The changing economy is opening up new ways to reconnect workers to their work and the profits from their work. These include traditional models such as self-employment and worker-owned cooperatives and new models of collaborative project-based work.

How do we change a dysfunctional, unsustainable and alienating system? By creating new ways of creating value and alternative models of cooperative work and ownership of the means of production.

Corporations and the state will have to adapt by offering workers more agency and ownership, or they will slide down the S-Curve to decay and collapse.

Section Three: The Core Skills and Values That Create Economic Value

What makes a worker a professional? In the conventional use of the word, professionalism means membership in a profession that is defined by a license to practice a specific trade.

I am using professionalism in a much broader sense, to describe those attributes that enable a worker to be productive in their own work and work effectively with others.

I have organized these attributes into eight core skills.

One would think that professionalism—broadly speaking, the ability to self-manage, to be accountable, to communicate clearly, learn new material and work easily with others—would be a core curriculum in higher education, given its critical importance in the world of work. One would be wrong.

Professionalism is not taught or even recognized as a subject worthy of being taught. Rather, the current educational system assumes that students learn these skills by osmosis or magic.

Critical skills are not taught directly in our educational system, but rather are assumed to be transferred via standard coursework. For example, self-learning to mastery is one of the essential skills needed to thrive in the emerging economy. The current system assumes that taking conventional courses teaches everyone to learn on one's own to the point of mastery. But like every other skill, the ability to self-learn to mastery must be explicitly taught and learned.

The current system assumes that classroom interactions impart the interpersonal skills needed to work effectively with others in the workplace, but it is quite possible to earn high marks in higher education and exit the system with poor interpersonal skills.

It is assumed that successfully navigating the institutions of higher education will impart professional skills: showing up on time, performing as promised, being accountable, and so on. Once again, this assumption is false: performing well in institutions of higher learning has no correlation to performance in the workplace. Observe how students in institutions of higher learning dress to go to class. Flip-flops, shorts and a tee shirt and the look of hardly taking a shower do not exude the aptitude necessary to be a professional.

If the higher education system does not explicitly teach these skills, students will not learn them, even if they excel in fulfilling the criteria of higher education—earning high marks on exams, etc.

The unspoken assumption of the current higher education system is that it is up to employers to teach their new employees. This is yet more evidence that higher education is completely out of touch with the real-world economy: in the real world, employers want new employees who are able to create value by profitably solving problems on day one.

Training people to be professional is a waste of time and money to enterprises facing a surplus of college-educated applicants.

The ultimate purpose of skills is to solve problems.

Problem-solving has become a cliché of sorts, and so we need to ask, what set of skills is required to profitably solve problems?

The set of necessary skills divides into two categories: hard skills in specific fields and soft skills that enable ownership of tasks and projects, systematic application of creativity and critical thinking, and professional standards of collaboration and conduct.

These two sets of skills are essential parts of human and social capital, hard and soft skills, experience and the ability to work productively with others. The ultimate purpose of education is to learn how to acquire human and social capital, and the ultimate purpose of human and social capital is mastery of the skills needed to solve problems.

Problem-solving and accountability have been generalized to the point that we need to specify what they actually mean. In my terminology, they mean taking ownership of tasks and projects, which is, accepting sole responsibility in the same manner as an owner.

Hard skills in science, technology, engineering and math are no longer enough: professional collaboration skills are increasingly essential even in workplaces that require engineering and scientific proficiency. The soft skills of collaboration, adaptability, creativity, entrepreneurism and professional accountability are core skills in every sector of the emerging economy.

The skills of professionalism are not learned by osmosis or magic; they must be taught as systematically as hard skills.

The skills needed to establish and maintain a livelihood in the emerging economy are the abilities to:

1. Learn challenging new material over one's entire productive life
2. Creatively apply newly-mastered knowledge and skills to a variety of fields
3. Be adaptable, responsible and accountable in all work environments
4. Apply a full spectrum of entrepreneurial skills to any task, that is, take ownership of one's work
5. Work collaboratively and effectively with others, both in person and remotely (online)
6. Communicate clearly and effectively in all work environments
7. Continually build human and social capital, that is, knowledge and networks

8. Possess a practical working knowledge of financial records and project management

If we step back and consider the soft skills needed to succeed in the emerging economy, we marvel that anyone believes the prevailing (but unspoken) assumption that coursework in the conventional fields of language, history, science and the humanities magically instills these essential skills in students via the regurgitation of mass-produced coursework.

Hard skills and soft skills of professionalism are only two-thirds of what's needed to establish and maintain a livelihood; a productive value system is just as essential as a set of skills.

Values as the Incubator of Economic Value

Our higher education system is based on the conviction that the primary impediment to universal prosperity is a lack of knowledge, which can be remedied with more education. This conviction cuts across ideological lines, as virtually everyone declares their belief in the economic value of education.

Since the key to prosperity is increasing productivity, the question becomes: does increasing a person's knowledge make them more productive? In some cases, the answer is clearly yes, but in other cases the answer is just as clearly no. Though it is politically sensitive, the difference between these two is based on the individual's value system and habits of behavior and thought.

The key traits needed not just to learn effectively but to apply the knowledge productively are self-discipline, the ability to focus for long periods of time, set aside current gratification for longer-term goals, persevere through difficulty and failure, work with others, accept responsibility and remain accountable at all times, along with a desire to achieve mastery in the skills required to secure a livelihood. All of this requires some self-knowledge and self-confidence.

The values needed to be successful at a job should be established early in life within the family and community. It is not unique to any one culture, society or faith; it is universal and accessible to all. Becoming a productive person is not limited to any one sector of the economy, or any one level of native intelligence. Though these values and habits are first acquired (or not acquired) in the family and community, they can be acquired later in life if the student is willing to learn.

A large body of research supports this common-sense connection between the core values acquired in the home and future prosperity. For example, the quantity and variety of books in the household is a better predictor of students' test scores than household income. Though wealthier families have the financial resources to offer their children more enrichment (after-school classes, for example), the immigrant experience in North America provides countless examples of families arriving with no financial assets who manage by dint of unceasing effort and thrift to lift their children into the prosperous class of highly productive citizens.

Conventional education assumes these values will be absorbed by osmosis; unfortunately there is little evidence for this osmosis and plenty of evidence that the gap between those with these values and those lacking these values widens in school rather than narrows.

Conventional education only benefits those who already possess the values and qualities that make them educable.

There are several factors in these differences. Educated parents clearly value education, as their own behavior reinforces the commitment to pursue higher education. Emotionally nurturing parents and caregivers instill the self-confidence needed to persevere through failure and criticism, and a culturally nurturing family provides the intellectual stimulation and human capital of early exposure to music, religion, the arts, positive ethnic identity and exposure to the social capital and cultural institutions.

There is little mystery about what separates accomplished, successful and prosperous families from those who struggle financially. The accomplished families are invariably led by parents who lead by example. Parents who play a musical instrument for pleasure reveal the payoff for the hard work of learning to play music, and those who serve on church or community committees illustrate the satisfaction and benefits of serving others. Parents who pursue interests and improve their own mastery outside of school or the workplace pass these values on to their children.

Additionally, though one would not know it from mainstream media coverage, financial wealth is still linked causally to the values of thrift and productive use of capital. On the next page there is a chart to illustrate my point that the habits of wealthy people lead to the development of human and social capital.

Remarkably, developing human and social capital does not necessarily require wealth or high income. Rather, a key determinant of human capital (psychological resilience, self-confidence and emotional intelligence) is the amount of nurturing time parents spend with their children and the parents' expectations of their children's behavior and values.

Mainstream financial and social success depends on networks and connections—social capital that is enabled by human capital. Those with more human capital are better able to take advantage of opportunities to build social capital than those with minimal human capital. The real advantage of attending an elite university is not the quality of the instruction per se but the opportunities to form friendships and professional connections that open doors unavailable to those outside the elite university. In other words, it is the social capital that counts, not the knowledge gained.

However, it requires an abundance of human capital to exploit these opportunities: the social skills of knowing how to dress and interact with accomplished people, knowing how to present (but not oversell) oneself, possessing the broad cultural knowledge necessary to understand the terms and contexts of conversations and situations, the self-confidence and humility needed to be a beginner, being a good listener, being able to recruit a mentor, gracefully accepting criticism, and so on.

Little of this human capital is related to one's educational level or classroom knowledge. If creativity is causally linked to the networking of creative people and new ideas, then one's network is more of a determinant of success than educational attainment per se – and research supports this contention.

The goal of human and social capital is to develop a network. The upper-class family is wealthy not just in assets, but in social capital, connections that open doors or solve problems in ways that are unavailable to the less well-connected.

If the family establishes basic human and social capital, then what role does education play, other than widening the existing gaps between those with more and less human/social capital? It is my contention that education can only increase productivity and the acquisition of human and social capital in two ways: (1) helping students learn how to learn, making the student the teacher; and (2) explicitly teaching the values, behaviors and habits that are needed to build human and social capital.

Investing in Ourselves

How do we acquire values and habits that manifest those values in our everyday lives? By putting them to practice every day of our lives, repeating the process over and over again.

When we utilize our willpower to organize ourselves into developing new processes (habits), we are investing in ourselves.

We can distill the dynamics of changing our habits to express positive values into five points:

1. It requires a daily application of self-discipline to form a new habit or replace a destructive habit with a more positive one.
2. If we spend our available willpower on an array of projects rather than on developing one new habit, we are unlikely to be able to persevere long enough to cement that new habit to the point where it is part of our routine.
3. The earlier in the day we apply our self-discipline to forming a new habit, the more success we will have simply because our reserves of willpower are most abundant early in the day.
4. Setting goals is easy. What's difficult is developing a process to reach the goal, and making that process into a habit that becomes part of our routine.
5. Once a process becomes a habit, we don't need to invest as much willpower in maintaining it.

The power to shape what we repeatedly do is the power to become more professional, improve our productivity, learn new material every day, and become a better mentor, more compassionate, a better listener—whatever we set as goals.

For example, as of this writing, one of the habits I am working on is getting enough sleep. Investing the appropriate amount of time into sleep is a key principle for attaining optimum health. Everyone is guilty of giving up some quality sleep time for something else, oftentimes attempting to 'make it up' later on. While you can't perfect your sleep schedule 100% percent of the time, getting sufficient sleep most of the time could be the solution to a number of troubles you currently face.

It's not surprising that many of the most productive people (artists, writers, scientists, etc.) often rise early and put in a solid morning of work without distraction. Given the nature of willpower and habit, that schedule makes good sense.

It is human nature to over-estimate our role in success and blame the system for our failures, and to focus on what we can't control rather than what we can control. Our economy is dysfunctional and structurally flawed; the centralized systems that dominate our economy are all on the diminishing return/decline phase of the S-Curve. I have often thought about writing books detailing these systemic flaws, but I thought who would read them? Who would take the time to analyze what I write and attempt to implement it? After all, as individuals, we can't fix these systemic failures. We have to live in the economy we have, not the one we hope will evolve in the future. What we do control is our own professionalism, values, integrity, authenticity, knowledge, skills and human and social capital.

Working Knowledge of Financial Records and Project Management

You may have noticed that seven of the eight core skills are soft skills and only the last one, a practical working knowledge of financial records and project management, is a hard skill. I included this hard skill because it is the foundation of assessing and organizing work that creates value or solves problems.

I did not use the word accounting because that word scares those who associate it with a difficult, tedious math-heavy slog. But the reality is that keeping accurate financial records and understanding what they communicate is necessary not just for large organizations but for bike repair shops, community groups, sole proprietors, etc.—every organization and enterprise.

The math required to maintain accurate financial records is simple addition and subtraction. It is not difficult.

The key characteristic of useful financial records is separating expenses and income into practical categories. Basic accounting software (i.e. QuickBooks Pro) enables users to attach a code to separate difficult categories of expenses and income. For example, utilities such as electrical bills and mobile phone charges might be coded 101. Restaurant and fast-food meals might be 102, and so on.

Humans are not wired to keep accurate accounts in their minds, and as a result, people with no accurate financial records are generally surprised to discover exactly how much they spend on groceries or eating out.

Why do accurate financial records matter? They are an essential component in understanding a problem well enough to actually solve it, and they are the foundation of effective project management.

If you come across an organization in chaos, you will inevitably find that the financial records are equally chaotic or that those in charge cannot understand the financial records and are thus unable to understand the organization's problems or the practicality of proposed solutions.

To solve problems, we must first understand the nature of the problem, and asses what resources are available to address the problem. Financial records help us accomplish both tasks. One part of our assessment is a cost-benefit analysis: how much will the proposed solution cost, and what is the opportunity cost of that solution? The opportunity cost is what was left undone because the available resources were devoted to the chosen project. Making the wrong choice and devoting resources to the wrong solution could doom the organization.

To calculate the opportunity cost, we must prepare a realistic budget for each option. Only then can we make an informed decision.

For those with no financial reporting experience, one place to start is your own household's income and expenses. Online courses and tutorials are resources available to anyone with an internet connection. The goal is to become familiar with income and expense sheets, also called profit and loss statements (P&L) and balance sheets which track assets and liabilities. These are the standard formats for reporting the finances of any organization.

Every project also has a financial reporting backbone: the budget, which compares projected expenses and income with actual expenses and income.

Ultimately, all work can be viewed as a project with a budget and a profit or loss. Everything from a home garden to a garage workshop to a global division can be constructively viewed as a project with a goal and a structure designed to reach that goal.

Developing a working knowledge of project management is thus the core skill needed to oversee and participate in any work, and understanding financial reporting is a key component in managing any project of any size.

As noted earlier, the two dynamics that characterize decline and eventual failure are diminishing returns and the S-Curve. Unproductive investments are those that absorb more and more resources while yielding less and less output: this is the classic definition of diminishing returns. But any project that wastes resources or makes inefficient use of resources is also guaranteeing diminishing returns.

The core of project management is establishing appropriate metrics to measure effectiveness, cost and to fully understand what the metrics are communicating. Financial reporting provided one metric, and measuring input and output is another. These are the core skills of good project management.

For example, if the project is designing a website for customers, the site's utility is measured not just by how much it cost to develop but by the quality and reliability of the user experience. A site whose functionality is limited or that crashes constantly is simply not effective: the output is substandard.

If a classroom project absorbs a tremendous amount of resources but does not result in improving measurable student learning, the project's output is substandard.

Effective project management requires:

1. Accountability

2. Transparency
3. Shared information and feedback (that is, no information hoarding is allowed)
4. Each piece of the project is small enough that failures can be resolved without threatening the progress of the entire project
5. Processes ensuring timely financial and output/results reporting and collaborative problem-solving are established and followed

Project management is ultimately about setting up and overseeing processes that get the work done. If a process isn't functioning effectively (it costs too much, results are substandard, accountability has been lost, participants are hoarding information, etc.) then it is reworked on the fly.

There are many resources for learning more about project management and virtually every organization offers fertile ground for practicing what you learn about managing cooperation, innovation and risk.

Your first and most important project is to manage and optimize your own learning and the accreditation of your skills, values and experience in creating value and solving problems.

Section Four: Higher Education Has Failed Students and the Economy

When I was in my second year of the Regional Economic and Social Development Master's program at the University of Massachusetts in Lowell, my classmates and I asked Dr. Chris Tilly, a famous economist and co-founder of the program we were studying in, what do we tell potential employers our title is? Since this was not a traditional economics graduate program, but a combination of economics, political science and sociology. Professor Tilly just looked at us with a smirk on his face and said, "Well, you can tell your employer you are an interdisciplinary problem solver". Although this kind of comment drew attention to the ability or lack thereof for this master's degree (which I never completed) to be able to assist me in obtaining a better job, it was this experience where I got the idea for Your Interdisciplinary Problem Solver. There was some truth to what Chris Tilly was saying when you look at it in light of the message of this book. We are going to focus on two basic themes here: The first is supply and demand: tens of millions of people have degrees now, and the supply of college graduates greatly exceeds the number of employers hiring workers on the basis of their college diploma.

The other reason is that higher education isn't preparing students to earn a livelihood in today's economy. This failing is systemic, meaning that it results from the structure of the system itself, rather than from defects in specific policies or programs.

The reality is the current system of higher education is broken and incapable of fixing itself. It has failed its most basic purpose, which is preparing students to earn a livelihood, and it depends on soaring student debt for funding. This is a double-whammy failure: higher education is burdening generations of students and their families with crippling debt while its product, a college diploma, has diminishing value in today's economy. A college diploma once guaranteed higher earnings and greater opportunity, but that is no longer true.

While the cost of college tuition has soared over 1,000% in a generation, a majority of recent college graduates are either jobless or working at jobs that do not require a college diploma; 53% of recent college graduates under the age of 25 are unemployed or doing work they could have done without going to college.

Student loans now exceed $1 trillion, with federal loans ballooning from $115 billion to over $700 billion in a few short years. Only 37% of freshman at four-year colleges graduate in four years and a mere 58% finally graduate in six years.

Defenders of higher education blame the economy for this poor showing but higher education is directly responsible for its failure to prepare graduates to earn a livelihood. A recent study from The Center for College Affordability and Productivity titled "From Wall Street to Wal-Mart," by Richard Vedder, Christopher Denhart, Matthew Denhart, Christopher Matgouranis and Jonathan Robe, explains that college education for many is a waste of time and money.

More than one-third of currently working college graduates are in jobs that do not require a degree. An essay by Vedder that complements the CCAP study reports that there are "one-third of a million waiters and waitresses with college degrees." The study says Vedder—distinguished professor of economics at Ohio University, an adjunct scholar at the American Enterprise Institute and director of CCAP—"was startled a year ago when the person he hired to cut down a tree had a master's degree in history, the fellow who fixed his furnace was a mathematics graduate, and, more recently, a TSA airport inspector was a recent college graduate."

Google is widely viewed as a bellwether of the new economy. It is noteworthy, then, that Google has found that academic success has little correlation with being productive in the workplace.

Doing well in college—earning high test scores and grades—has no measurable correlation with becoming an effective worker or manager. This is incontrovertible evidence that the entire higher education system is detached from the real economy: excelling in higher education has little discernible correlation to real-world skills or performance.

What is striking about these runaway costs and failure to prepare students for today's economy is the stunning lack of accountability: the higher education system continues to maintain it is cost-effective and successful even as evidence piles up that it is unaffordable and obsolete.

This lack of accountability and runaway pricing are hallmarks of a cartel, a quasi-monopoly that offers an illusory veneer of competition to mask its cartel nature. In the present system, colleges maintain a government-granted monopoly on accreditation: if you want a college degree, you have to pay the cartel its price, regardless of the education's quality or value. There is no accountability for the poor product because students have nowhere else to go for a diploma but the cartel.

Over 25% of students at major state colleges are already taking classes online, courses which are almost free to deliver as they require no classroom, campus or live instructor. In a competitive, accountable system, we would expect these savings to be passed onto students. Instead, tuition and fees continue rising every year, often at double-digit rates.

The double-whammy of ever-higher costs and declining value for the product (a college degree) creates a no-win dilemma for today's college-age students and millions of older workers who hope that going back to college will benefit their careers: the current system has demonstrably failed, but there are no alternatives except to forego a college diploma and hope that this won't damage one's career prospects.

We can summarize the failure of secondary and higher education in two key points:

1. The education system prepares students to advance to the next level of higher education, not to create value and profitably solve problems in the real economy.
2. The goal of the education system is for students to obtain a credential rather than skills that are essential in the real economy. The credential is seen as a proxy for knowledge or even wisdom; but a proxy of knowledge is not the same as knowledge embedded in human and social capital.

The credentials of higher education are thus largely worthless in the real economy, as proxies don't create value or solve problems; the emerging economy needs workers with practical skills and professionalism.

The next section lays out a practical path between the dead-end choices of a high-cost, low-value college diploma and not pursuing any accreditation: it's called accredit yourself.

This practical path combines one old idea, one new idea, one largely forgotten idea and one key insight into today's economy.

The old idea is networking. The advent of social-media networks made this old idea new to some, but the idea that the best way to get a job is to network has been around for a long time.

This book will explain how to network effectively. Everything that people refer to as networking is not of equal value; much of what passes for networking has little value in terms of learning new skills and finding a job.

The new idea is accredit yourself. I will have much more to say about this, but one key piece is another old idea: mastery.

The largely forgotten idea is the essential role of personal values in creating economic value, either as an employee or in your own business. I have distilled these down into the eight essential skills of professionalism described in the previous section.

The person every employer wants is one who can learn whatever needs to be learned and solve problems with integrity, accountability, diligence, and do so while working effectively and easily with others.

The person who knows how to master new skills and apply them effectively with integrity, accountability and diligence will be able to get the job done, regardless of their major in college or the number of diplomas they earned. Indeed, as we have noted, college diplomas have little correlation to being effective on the job.

For those pursuing certain careers, a college diploma is still a requirement. We will discuss ways to lower the cost of obtaining that degree so that a lifetime of debt (student loans) can be avoided.

One key component of this path is to start seeking to accredit yourself on day one of college, rather than waiting until graduation day to start preparing yourself to get a job.

In the conventional higher education timeline, the college student spends four to six years in an extension of adolescence, devoting himself to coursework and "the college experience" while working a few hours on campus or in a low-skill service job off campus. After four or five years of attending classes and investing tens of thousands of dollars in tuition, fees, books, room and board, etc., the student exits the higher education system with a diploma and then starts the process of finding a job in his chosen field; for others, multiple degrees will be necessary (for example, physicians), and for those in neither category, higher education must be viewed as one part of accrediting yourself.

The key insight into today's economy is understanding how you will accredit yourself.

Although you may be itching to learn more about accrediting yourself, it's important to first understand why the higher education system is obsolete.

The Old System: Systemic Scarcity of Media and Knowledge

We need to start with the historical roots of the current system, which arose from a profound scarcity of knowledge and instruction. In the ancient world, storing information was extremely expensive. Even after Gutenberg's printing press made mass-produced books available, books remained expensive; only a wealthy household could afford to buy more than a few books.

Instruction was similarly limited. Instruction in universities was often on person reading a text aloud to a classroom of students; this is the source of Cambridge University's longstanding academic rank of Reader.

The scarcity and high cost of written media led to the primacy of the oral lecture, as the only way to share knowledge was to concentrate students in one small geographic area to hear these lectures.

Despite the ubiquity of relatively inexpensive books, higher education in the 20th century remained essentially unchanged from the medieval model of students gathering to hear lectures drawn from large libraries. This high-cost structure insured that universities were elite institutions, finishing schools for the upper-class and a narrow channel of meritocracy for the best and brightest of the lower classes. In 1940, only 5% of adults had a college diploma.

World War II and the Advent of the Factory Model

The advent of global war in 1941 required a rapid expansion of industry and managerial skills on an unprecedented scale. Unlike previous wars, oil, technology, industrial production, advanced research and management of these complex systems became paramount in World War II, and in response the federal government ramped up the nation's small elitist system of higher education into a vast factory of universities and colleges producing millions of educated workers to serve the emerging knowledge-based economy.

This factory model was based on the principles of mass production: college students attended the same lectures as hundreds of others and studied the same textbooks as thousands of others. The system of accrediting each college created an illusion of parity between institutions: while an Ivy League diploma, any bachelor's degree was deemed adequate proof of academic achievement.

This factory model yielded a three-part system: the traditional elite of academia, research and the professional schools (that is, graduate and doctoral programs), mass-produced four-year bachelor's degrees, and a two-year community college system that served two roles: as preparation for a bachelor's degree and as a vocational school.

The need for white-collar managerial workers exceeded the output of college graduates in the 1950s and 60s, so the fundamentals of supply and demand favored college graduates, who found good-paying jobs relatively quickly and opportunities for advancement relatively expansive.

Colleges expanded quickly, using federal and state funds to construct sprawling campuses. Costs were held down by modest salaries and benefits for non-tenured instructors and flat management structures.

In effect, a hodge-podge system tossed together in a national crisis became institutionalized. This is best revealed by this question: if we could start from scratch now, how would we design a cost-effective, responsive, accountable system of higher education?

The Higher Education Cartel

The basic structure of higher education can be summarized in eight points:

1. As noted above, higher education is a legacy system based on the scarcity of recorded knowledge (printed and other media) and lectures.

Both recorded knowledge and lectures are now essentially free and readily available to everyone with a digital device (i.e. khanacademy.org, udemy.org, youtube.com, etc.)

2. The current higher education model is a factory composed of lectures and mass-distributed coursework/tests. The student moves down the assembly line, attending the same lectures as other students, reading the same materials and taking the same tests. When the student receives a passing grade in a quasi-arbitrary number of courses, he or she is accredited, that is, issued a diploma.
3. In terms of its financial structure, higher education is a cartel-like system that limits its product (accredited instruction) and restricts its output (credentials, diplomas). This creates an artificial scarcity.
4. The cartel's basic mechanism of maintaining non-competitive pricing is to enforce an artificial scarcity of credentials. The cartel's control of a product that is in high demand (college diplomas) frees it from outside competition and free-market price discovery, enabling it to charge customers (students) an extraordinary premium for a product whose value is entirely scarcity-based.

This is the very definition of a rent-seeking cartel, a cartel that extracts premiums solely on the basis of an artificial scarcity. By their very nature, rent-seeking cartels are exploitive and parasitic, drawing resources from those who can least afford to pay high premiums and misallocating capital that could have been invested in productive social investments.

The term rents in this context means that the cartel collects a premium without providing any corresponding additional value.

Since the higher education cartel is the sole provider of accreditation (college diplomas), it is unaccountable for its failure to prepare its customers (students) for productive employment in the emerging economy. If a diploma is portrayed as essential, students must pay the cartel even if the cartel's product is ineffective and obsolete.

5. The four-year college system is profoundly disconnected from the economy. That the cartel's product has little practical application is not considered a factor in the value of the product (diploma), a credential that is a proxy for knowledge rather than proof of practical knowledge.
6. The present system of higher education is unaffordable for all but the wealthy. The cartel's solution to its high prices, $1 trillion in student loan debt, is a crushing burden on both individuals and society at large.
7. The higher education cartel is an intrinsically elitist force, as its survival as a rent-seeking cartel is based on limiting what is now essentially free: knowledge and instruction. In other words, the higher education cartel charges an extraordinary premium for a free product.
8. The only way the higher education cartel can continue to charge a premium for nearly-free products is to actively mystify its product (by attributing secular sanctity to its diplomas) and promote an artificial value for this product using public relations and political lobbying. In other words, the higher education cartel operates on the same principles as other parasitic cartels: it depends on the government to enforce the scarcity of its product, and it uses public relations to mask its cartel structure and systemic failure to fulfill its stated purpose.

Charging a Premium for Elitist Social Connections: The Spoils System

It has long been understood that the value proposition in attending an elite university is not the instruction but the social connections forged with children of the elite, influential professors and alumni. This can be summarized by the expression, "it's who you know, not what you know." The unspoken assumption is that a great many people are equally qualified for lucrative positions in finance and governance, and the selection process is based less on talent and creativity than on being socially connected to those with the power to hire or introduce candidates to other influential people.

The rising value of elitist social connections reflects a system in which opportunity is diminishing—a system that is getting poorer, not wealthier.

The recognition that social connections mean more than merit, hard work, creativity and talent fuels parents' desperation to get their children into elite universities. But since an increasing number of others are playing the same manic game of getting their kids into the "right" kindergarten or prep school, enrichment activities, test preparation program, etc., this pathway leaves more disappointed parents and students ill-prepared for earning a livelihood outside the privileged spoils-system.

This system enables ever-higher prices for access to elite universities while the purported value of the access declines as an ever-larger number of graduates seek the same few slots in the spoils system.

Pursuing acceptance to an elite university with the goal of securing a slot in the spoils system is guaranteed to disappoint the vast majority of students and their parents, as the number of slots in the various elite institutions is so much smaller than the number of qualified candidates.

Approaching higher education with the goal of acquiring mastery of productive knowledge and the eight essential skills is the higher-value path. This is the essence of accredit yourself.

The Economy Changed; the Factory Model Didn't

The U.S. economy has changed in fundamental ways since the heyday of the factory model of higher education in the 1950s and 60s. In that era, the U.S. maintained a near-monopoly on capital and industry as war-ravaged Europe and Japan were still rebuilding their shattered economies. The rapid expansion of the consumer economy demanded an equally rapid expansion in the white-collar workforce of managers and marketers, and those with college diplomas were a scarce commodity who could command a premium on the labor market. Healthcare was cheap and economic growth robust; overhead costs were low and it behooved companies to offer stable employment, low-cost benefits and pension plans.

The system had another important feature: it was assumed that employers would provide new college graduates on-the-job training to prepare them for productive work. A college diploma was evidence of the student's perseverance and ability to navigate institutional processes, not his readiness to produce value in the real-world economy. A college degree was a stamp that enabled the holder to enter the white-collar workforce: a proxy for knowledge rather than proof of knowledge. The school or subject was less important than the accreditation (diploma) itself.

These employer-operated training programs were often lengthy and comprehensive; in effect, employers shouldered the enormously expensive task of transforming a green college graduate with little or no actual job-related skills into a productive employee.

The 1970s upended many aspects of this high-growth era. Energy crises bled the economy of efficiency and purchasing power, and the era of high wages for low-skill factory work gave way to the first waves of global competition, automation, computerization and robotics.

This structural shift from industrial to post-industrial employment fueled a systemic need for workers with advanced knowledge of computers, software and related technical skills, as well as a secondary pool of workers able to deploy these new technologies in every sector of the economy: defense, design, communications, marketing, human resources, government, finance, engineering, etc.

The factory model could adjust to this new need by expanding curricula in these new fields while keeping the traditional departments and schools on a continued expansionary track.

Demographics played a role as well; the 60+ million baby boomers that had begun entering college in the mid-60s reached its college-age apogee in the 1970s.

This legacy system of mass-produced college diplomas made the transition from an industrial economy to a post-industrial economy because tens of millions of college graduates were absorbed into four expanding sectors: the financialization industry (the so-called FIRE economy of finance, insurance and real estate), the consumer-driven sectors of sales and marketing, the government funded fields of healthcare and education and the digital technology industries.

Those with advanced degrees found high-level jobs within academia itself, government or industry.

All of these industries have reached the point of saturation and diminishing returns: financialization has hollowed out the economy and triggered systemic instability; sales and marketing are being revolutionized by digital technologies; the enormous resources being poured into healthcare and education feed vested interests while yielding fewer measurable results, and the digital technologies are automating not just engineering and management in every sector but the very process of engineering advances.

Costly on-the-job training programs have vanished as enterprises are too stretched to invest time and capital in training new employees, knowing that competitors may well poach them once their training is complete. Employers in today's economy want employees who can start working productively on day one, not six months from now after extensive training. In today's era of global competition, lavishing months of costly training on domestic workers makes no financial sense when lower cost employees with job-readiness skills can be hired by the corporation's overseas operations.

The factory model of higher education has failed to make the transition to the emerging economy, and indeed, cannot make the transition as it is structurally disconnected from today's economy.

Degree Inflation and the False Promise of Specialization

Not only does a general education no longer prepare students for work in the new economy: there is no longer an insatiable need for ever greater number of advanced degree specialists and PhDs in every field.

Many PhDs have been reduced to what academic ronins. Ronin is the term to classify a masterless and landless samurai in feudal Japan. In this case, an academic ronin is a highly educated teacher or researcher who cannot get a permanent tenured position within academia as the number of qualified candidates far exceeds the number of jobs. It is not uncommon to find hundreds of PhDs applying for one tenure-track position.

As with all fields in today's economy, the competition is global. This imbalance between the huge number of people with advanced degrees and the small number of secure positions leaves the majority with few choices other than an insecure career of wandering from institution to institution on short-term contracts—hence the reference to masterless and landless samurai in feudal Japan (ronin).

The structural imbalance between the rising number of highly educated jobseekers and a stagnating number of positions requiring their level of education is also visible in the professions: law, architecture, MBAs, etc. Media accounts of attorneys losing jobs that paid $170,000 and after a lengthy job search eventually landing a $40,000-per-year position are increasingly common.

The higher education system consistently overpromises and under-delivers on real-world results. The gap between its rosy public-relations claims and the experiences of graduates has widened to the point that the system's PR has lost credibility to those who examine the post-graduation jobs data.

Higher education's self-serving solution to the widening disconnect between the promised benefits of additional degrees and the stark reality of today's job market has been to over-promise the benefits of ever more specialized degrees. Where a degree in Marketing was once sufficient, now there are Master's programs in Pharmaceutical Marketing. Management degrees (the ubiquitous MBA) are now subdividing into Casino Management, and so on.

The trend exemplifies the profound disconnect between higher education and the emerging economy: as higher education narrows its focus on increasingly specific jobs, the economy is blurring the lines between such narrow categories of jobs and creatively destroying or reworking entire industries. Rather than demanding more specialized knowledge of siloed jobs, the economy is demanding collaborative work across multiple fields and disciplines. The more specialized the education, the more likely it will be outdated, bypassed or undervalued by a dynamic economy and collaboratively developed projects, knowledge bases and skills.

In effect, higher education is predicting what jobs will be in demand (or still exist) five, ten and twenty years in the future by promoting specialized degrees. Is there any evidence that higher education has the tools to accurately predict what jobs will be in demand in the future?

This increasing specialization of degrees simply gives human resources departments a perfect reason to reject job seekers: sorry, your degree is in casino management, we need someone who can manage software implementation.

If you wanted to doom students to economic dead-ends, you'd funnel them into narrow, specialized degrees—exactly what the higher education system is doing.

Legacy systems fail for a number of reasons, including loss of adaptability, higher costs coupled with diminishing returns, institutional sclerosis, vested interests incapable of reforming themselves out of a job, mission creep, loss of the original purpose, and so on.

But the deeper reason is that the legacy system itself is the impediment to progress; as a result, even modest reforms trigger collapse of a system that has become obsolete.

The economy of the 2010s is undergoing a change just as dramatic and wrenching as the transition from industrial to post-industrial. The economy—and competition for capital, skills, goods and services—is global. Overhead costs such as healthcare have soared, making hiring workers an expensive proposition. With roughly 40% of the workforce holding a college diploma, the scarcity of college-educated workers has been replaced by a surplus of workers with university degrees.

Granting more advanced degrees does not magically create positions for those holding freshly issued diplomas. Instead, degree inflation is at work: what once required a high school diploma now requires a bachelor's degree, what once required a bachelor's degree now requires a master's degree, and so on.

As corporate and government human resources departments have increasingly fenced off even low-level jobs as requiring a college diploma, a bachelor's degree is becoming the entry-level minimum, replacing the high school diploma. Further up the food chain, master's degrees are also in surplus, pushing many ambitious youth into PhD programs, in the hope that a PhD will guarantee a high-paying job. Alas, as noted above, there is a growing surplus of people with PhDs. Some claim the unemployment rate for PhDs is very low, but these surveys do not measure under-employment, that is, did the PhD take a position that only required a lesser degree?

The higher education cartel is perfectly happy to encourage degree inflation (at enormous expense to students, of course), but this zeal for issuing student-loan funded diplomas fails to address two structural disparities: the gap between the skills needed to prosper in the emerging economy and the skills colleges are providing students, and the widening income/wealth/education gap between the wealthy and the non-wealthy.

As higher education costs soar, the divide between wealthy and poor families widens as non-wealthy students are forced to become debt-serfs to pay for college. A system that forces poor households to shoulder student loans for decades in return for marginal-utility college degrees is not just immoral, it is recklessly predatory. Yet this is the system higher education supports and defends.

There is a profound disconnect between the higher education cartel and what higher education should cost in a world where information, instruction and knowledge have fallen to the cost of bandwidth, that is, near-zero. What was once costly and scarce (knowledge and instruction) is now nearly free and abundant, readily available on any digital device anywhere in the world with a connection to the web. There is no need to concentrate students in a campus with a library; every web-connected digital device is a library and university combined.

In essence, the foundation of higher education has been completely upended: knowledge and instruction, once costly and scarce, are now abundant and nearly free, giving you the ability to accredit yourself. The only pricing power left to the higher education cartel is the artificial scarcity of credentials.

That is not the power of a productive system; it is the power of a parasitic, predatory system.

A Credential/Degree Does Not Verify Mastery

Let's start by listing what various forms of accreditation actually verify.

A diploma issued by a professional school (nursing, dental hygiene, architecture, law, etc.) is presumed to prepare the graduate to pass the licensing exam that enables them to practice in their field. This is a model that functions because the goal is to prepare the student for an objective appraisal of their knowledge, and there is a feedback loop: schools whose graduates fail the licensing exam in great numbers will eventually lose students based on their poor performance.

Unfortunately, this model of objective testing of graduates' knowledge and feedback for poor performance by the college is limited to professional schools. In my view, this model should be extended to the entire higher education system. This professional system of verification and feedback is the foundation of the accrediting yourself model.

A non-professional-school four-year bachelor's degree verifies that the student completed the requirements of the minimum number of courses to graduate. The diploma does not verify the knowledge the student learned or the critical skills he acquired, if any, in the coursework, nor does it verify the student learned how to learn, that is, that he has the ability to be his own teacher.

The degree does nothing to verify that the student has the requisite core values needed for gainful employment, for example, integrity, professionalism and accountability. The higher education credential is a proxy for knowledge rather than proof of practical knowledge.

Given the wide spectrum of quality in college coursework, a bachelor's degree offers essentially no useful verification of skills, values or knowledge. The only trait that a bachelor's degree verifies is the student's ability to navigate (or game) an institution of higher education long enough and successfully enough to gather the minimum number of credits for graduation.

Credentials prepare students not to create value in the real economy but for acceptance to the next level in the accreditation bureaucracy.

A master's degree offers an equivalent dearth of useful verification; if the master's program required a thesis, the graduate's thesis offers some evidence of the student's ability to write clearly and succinctly (assuming the thesis is solely the student's work, something that is difficult to verify in an age of copy-and-paste and academic ghostwriters).

A doctorate (PhD) verifies the graduate's knowledge of the field and their ability to perform independent research. The PhD degree does not verify the graduate's teaching ability or any other soft skill, or their professionalism and values, though some of these traits may be visible to the graduate's faculty advisors. But the PhD itself does not verify anything but the graduate's knowledge and research/written communication capabilities.

In professions such as architecture, dental hygiene and law, a diploma is not enough in most states to begin practicing in the real world; graduates are required to pass a test that verifies their knowledge of the profession's essentials.

These professional exams verify the graduate's basic body of knowledge, but do not verify the graduate's values, ability to work effectively with others, or their general competence in the actual practice of their profession.

The only way to verify working knowledge and professionalism is to provide a multi-year supervised apprenticeship of on-the-job training. Trade union apprenticeships are a traditional example of multiyear on-the-job training programs, as are residency programs for doctors and nurses.

Physicians must actually practice their profession under the supervision of experienced physicians in a multi-year residency program before they are licensed to practice medicine. This long training and apprenticeship verifies not just their knowledge and experience but also offers an opportunity to verify their values and soft skills of communication, collaboration with others, etc.

In the armed forces, soldiers, sailors and marines must verify their knowledge and professional abilities on active duty to advance in rank.

This brief overview reveals just how little useful information about a graduate is verified by a college degree—even an advanced degree. Obtaining a credential can be gamed, gaining practical knowledge and professionalism cannot. A proxy of knowledge and skills is not the same as practical knowledge and skills or professionalism. This is the core failure of the higher education cartel.

Given that the ideal job candidate, regardless of the field or position, has learned how to master new knowledge quickly and applies high professional values and standards to every task, we can see just how low-value a college degree is in terms of assessing and selecting employees.

Since a college degree only verifies the graduate's ability to navigate a higher education institution, the task of verifying everything of importance and value to employers, customers and colleagues falls to the student. This is why it's essential to acquire the eight essential soft skills that create economic value and to learn how to accredit yourself.

The Accredit Yourself Model

In the Accredit Yourself model, students earn credentials by passing exams that demonstrate their grasp of knowledge—the method of demonstrating knowledge in professions such as medicine, dental hygiene, architecture and law.

Though the formal Accredit Yourself does not yet exist, all of the pieces are already in place. The opportunity to learn and accredit your own knowledge and experience are available to everyone with an internet connection and a digital device.

To understand the process of accrediting yourself, let's briefly review how the Accredit Yourself model works.

There are four broad technology-enabled solutions that can free higher education from its current cartel limitations:

1. *Accredit the student, not the school.* By accrediting the student rather than the institution, we remove control of the credential supply and pricing from the cartel and establish the value of what the student has mastered by objective standards.

    The concept of accrediting the student, not the school is well-established in the professions. Obtaining a law, architecture or dental hygiene degree does not confer the right to practice those professions in the real world; one must demonstrate mastery of the field by passing a lengthy examination.

How difficult would it be to transfer this concept to all students in higher education? In the digital age, there is no technological or cost barrier to establishing a largely automated online procedure for taking exams and making the results available to prospective employers or collaborators.

2. *Structure learning such that it no longer depends on large physical campuses and costly administration.* Higher education has two claims of value: one, the issuance of credentials (diplomas), and two, the claim that the product (instruction) can only be gained in a classroom managed by a high-cost bureaucracy.

   In the digital age, learning is no longer tethered to large physical campuses and expensive administration. Anyone with an internet connection and a digital device has access to essentially unlimited knowledge, lessons and tutorials.

3. *Tailor the curriculum to the needs of the real-world emerging economy and the methods of learning to the individual student.*

   The value proposition in education is no longer the live lecturer who assigns the same material to hundreds of students or the administration of the factory model of education; it is the assembly of free learning tools that fit the needs of the real emerging economy and the individual student. Classes no longer need be scheduled and attended during working hours; digital courses are available 24 hours a day, 7 days a week year-round.

4. *Eliminate the artificial scarcity of admissions and accreditation.* The Accredit Yourself model eliminates this artificial scarcity and the elite-controlled spoils system it creates. Accrediting yourself is open to all; has no artificial scarcity, no spoils system and no elites.

Not Just Cheaper, but Better

There are three key technologies in the Accredit Yourself model:

1. *Digital media*. Everything that can be digitized is nearly free to distribute.
2. *Adaptive learning*, where software tailors curricula, lessons and methods to each individual student
3. *Massively networked participants*

Digital media is self-explanatory; what needs to be mentioned is the extraordinary willingness of people to share their knowledge—not just massively open online courses from enterprises such as the Khan Academy, Coursera, Udemy, Lynda.com or Saylor.com, but from the university of Youtube. This vast library of lessons is expanding daily, and includes instruction on everything from sewing a button to digital logic design.

Adaptive learning is not just a cheaper way of learning—it is clearly a better way of learning. As Salman Khan, founder of the Khan Academy observed in the beginning of his book, *The One World School House*, "there would be no shame or stigma in progressing slowly, no dreaded moment when the class has to move on." This is but one example of the benefits of adaptive learning.

Massively networked participants fuels innovation because it's not just the coursework that is open to everyone—the entire spectrum of data, experimental results, critiques and "best practices" is available to every participant in the accrediting yourself model.

We are already accustomed to accrediting restaurants, hotels and a host of other services via user reviews; the web offers the possibility of assembling one's own accreditation from trustworthy sources whose own credibility can also be verified.

This is why some types of networking are far more successful than others. We'll discuss both of these applications in more detail later.

Should I Get a College Degree?

The stark reality that the value of college diplomas is declining raises pressing and difficult-to-answer questions for young people: should I get a college degree? If I don't have a college degree, how will I get a career/job?

It raises similar questions of older workers: should I go back to school to earn another degree?

To answer these questions, we need to break them down into smaller inquiries.

1. Do you want to enter a profession that requires a degree and a licensing certification, such as medicine, law or architecture, or a trade that requires a two-year certificate and a licensing certification?

These questions are impossible to answer without directly experiencing the field first-hand. If you think you might enjoy being a nurse, dental hygienist or physician, then volunteer in a hospital for a summer. If you think you might enjoy being an attorney, then volunteer for a summer in a law office. There is no substitute for experiencing the day-to-day routines and tasks of whatever profession interests you.

Thinking you might like a field is not the same as knowing you like the field based on months of hands-on experience. Many people who reckoned they'd like practicing law and who earn a law degree without ever having worked in a real-world law firm discover to their surprise they dislike the actual practice of law.

Thinking you will enjoy the salary and status of a job is not the same as actually enjoying the day-to-day practice of the job.

After spending a few months working in your field of interest—a hospital, law office, architecture firm, restaurant kitchen, farm, kindergarten classroom, bakery, auto body shop, graphic design firm, pharmacy, biotech lab, social services office, etc.—you will know if that's the sort of work you want to do for years or decades. You may well discover if it's a good fit for you within the first few days.

2. Is there an oversupply of qualified people in this field?

This question matters because the last thing you want is to devote years of your life and tens of thousands of dollars for a credential or license that is in oversupply, that is, the number of qualified people far exceeds the number of job openings in the field.

Supply and demand are in constant flux. As demand for specific skills rises in a stagnating economy, more people seek the training as a way of insuring a secure job. If enough people flood into the field, the number of qualified people eventually exceeds the number of jobs.

This reality forces every student to look into a crystal ball and predict what the job market will look like in their chosen field four, five and ten years down the road.

Though this may seem impossible to do, talking to people in the field and in training programs will enable you to make an informed assessment.

Many professions that once absorbed all graduates such as law are now oversupplied with qualified applicants. As degree inflation has become the norm, fields in which as master's degree once practically guaranteed a job are now plagued by an oversupply of people with master's degrees. Even a doctorate (PhD) is no longer a guarantee, as many PhDs are underemployed or working as academic ronins in insecure positions.

3. Do you want to work for large-scale organizations such as a corporation or state agency with bureaucratic human resources departments that see college degrees as sufficient credentials to apply for a job?

If so, then you will need that passport called a degree. Your challenge then becomes 1) doing so without going into debt and 2) structuring your college years around gaining the eight essential skills and accrediting yourself so you're actually prepared to create value and profitably solve problems when you exit college.

The only way to go to college without going into debt is to either obtain a full scholarship, a benefit that is increasingly rare, or attend a state university while living at home or with a relative working part-time.

Having a part-time job is not a detriment, it is an enormous asset, as a part-time job in your field of interest will give you invaluable experience to learn, build networks and accredit yourself.

If paying work for beginners in your chosen field is scarce, the next best thing is to work for someone with the skills and social capital to mentor you and provide opportunities that are only available to those within his/her professional network. Such work could be unrelated to your field of interest; as we saw in Section One, those with social capital and the willingness to learn can acquire hard skills.

4. Does your field of interest offer jobs in small enterprises without human resources departments, that is, enterprises where what you can do matters more than what proxy of knowledge (diploma) you have?

A great many jobs can be learned and mastered without formal diploma programs. Small enterprises are by necessity, organizations where the more you do the more influence and earnings you can potentially gain, as there is not enough money lying around to pay under-performers, whether they have a degree or not.

Do your best to perform at a high professional level, creating value and solving problems along the way as this is what every enterprise wants and needs, and the more advanced enterprises have realized that a proxy knowledge (a degree) does not necessarily mean the graduate has the hard and soft skills to create value and solve problems.

A degree doesn't guarantee there will be a job for every graduate, and that not having a degree doesn't preclude having a successful and fulfilling career. Those who want to become licensed professionals will have to complete the professional training. Those who want to work in large-scale corporations and state agencies with bureaucratic human resources departments may be expected to have a degree of some sort just to apply for a position.

But these highly bureaucratic organizations are precisely the ones most likely to be disrupted going forward, because the gains to be reaped by replacing their inefficiencies are the lowest hanging fruit.

A relatively few professions (such as physicians) are guaranteed jobs by dint of certification and licensing. For the vast majority of workers, establishing a livelihood may or may not require a college degree or licensing, but it will certainly require the professionalism and skills required to work productively in a small enterprise where the work you do in creating value and solving problems is your accreditation.

Rather than ask, should I go to college or not, the more insightful question is, what do I need to do to prepare myself to create value and profitably solve problems in small enterprises where the work I do is my accreditation in my selected field?

Summary: Putting the Accrediting Yourself Model to Work for You

The higher education cartel promotes four fallacies that enable it to siphon hundreds of billions of dollars in revenue:

1. That a proxy of knowledge (a diploma or credential) is equivalent to practical working knowledge and human capital; it is not.
2. That the solution to the declining value of a bachelor's degree is getting additional degrees, that is, degree inflation. But obtaining more proxies of knowledge does not prepare a student to create value and profitably solve problems in the real economy.
3. That knowledge and skills acquired outside the higher education cartel are of little value because the cartel did not issue a proxy (credential) of that knowledge.
4. That there is no need to teach the essential values and skills of professionalism; these are magically acquired by osmosis in factory model classrooms.

The claims of the higher education cartel are strikingly Orwellian, as each claim is the reversal of reality.

The cartel's proxies of knowledge (credentials) are intrinsically low-value because they do not objectively verify any actual acquisition of knowledge or skills.

Obtaining additional proxies of knowledge (at enormous expense) is equally low-value for the same reasons.

Knowledge acquired outside the cartel is not worthless—it is the foundation of the professionalism and practical skills that are valuable in the real economy.

Professionalism is not gained by osmosis or magic; it must be learned like any other skill.

While some professions still require degrees, the value of college diplomas outside these specific professions is declining because the diplomas do not actually verify the student acquired practical knowledge or skills.

It is thus up to each person who isn't in a licensed profession to accredit themselves by demonstrating objective, verifiable evidence of mastery and professionalism.

In the age of the University of Youtube, knowledge is essentially free. The process of acquiring economically useful mastery of a subject requires a structured curriculum, and the ideal structured curriculum is one designed to fit the aptitudes and learning preferences of each individual.

The tools to design such a curriculum for ourselves are available to anyone willing to do the work.

Just as learning is now untethered from the higher education cartel, accreditation is now available to everyone.

Section Five: Accrediting Yourself

The Need to Accredit Yourself

Let's take a moment to summarize our findings:

1. The higher education system is a self-serving cartel that charges astronomical prices for its diminishing-value products (that is, college diplomas) by enforcing an artificial scarcity of credentials in an era of essentially free knowledge.
2. The higher education system does not recognize or teach the critical skills and core values of professionalism needed to secure a livelihood (get a job or start a business) in today's economy.

3. College degrees do not verify the graduate's knowledge, skills, talents or core values. The goal within the current system is earning credentials, not actual knowledge/skills. A credential is not knowledge; it is a proxy with no verifiable value.
4. An alternative system, accrediting yourself and the University of YouTube, is emergent but not yet issuing credentials (accredited degrees).

This means it's up to each student to learn on their own what college doesn't provide: the eight essential skills/values of professionalism and the ability to create value and solve problems.

Since a college degree accredits essentially nothing about the student's professionalism, knowledge, skills or human capital, we must each accredit ourselves by demonstrating these attributes in the real world.

Fortunately, a vast spectrum of knowledge is available for free (or low cost) online, and many people are ready and willing to help you for free.

The Necessary Steps to Accrediting Yourself

The core of Accredit Yourself requires first acquiring the eight essential skills of professionalism and whatever hard skills are needed to be effective in your chosen field, and then verifying your mastery of the skills by completing projects that demonstrate your working knowledge, creativity, experience and ability to learn, solve problems and work with others. The next step is to assemble accounts from trustworthy colleagues, employers, advisors and peers with direct knowledge of your contributions that demonstrate your experience, abilities, skills and core values.

The last step is to share these credentials with networks of people, agencies and enterprises that are active in your chosen field.

One way to think about the process of accrediting yourself is to imagine that you're filling in all the blanks that are filled by professional verification processes such as residencies for doctors and nurses and apprenticeship programs for union tradespeople.

Put yourself in the shoes of a potential employer, client or customer: what would you need to know about a person before entrusting them with key tasks?

You'd want to know that they have demonstrated they can get the job done by completing similar projects. You'd want to know they've shown they can learn new material quickly, that they possess the emotional intelligence and maturity to respond positively to fair criticism, and that they've demonstrated the ability to collaborate effectively with others, both in person and online. You'd want trustworthy sources to confirm the candidate's personal integrity and professionalism. I will not address here the idea that employers want to see that an employee can effectively problem solve. You may read a lot of online articles saying this is the case, but what they don't make clear is that creative problem solving is mainly only possible on the part of those in positions of management in a lot of big highly bureaucratic companies and in small organizations what can a low-level staff member do to solve the problem that everyone else around him or her has resigned? It is up to the manager of the organization to hire more staff or ask his remaining loyal staff member what he or she thinks should happen? A lot of customer service jobs say they want people that can solve problems but what they really want is someone who will deal with an unsatisfied customer and give the customer service supervisor breathing room to take care of administrative duties and enjoy a nice long lunch without the stresses of yet another angry customer.

This is the real reason why the process of accrediting yourself is so important. You want to lower the risk of hiring you to do a high-skill, high-value task so you can avoid a current trend in the economy which is missing out on your own skill building and self-actualization because you lack the solid verification of key attributes while temp agencies and companies keep calling you to fill their call centers that they cannot keep consistently staffed because of high turnover. You cannot just rest your future on what is written on your resume/CV (curriculum vitae) for a number of reasons.

One is that resumes can be inflated or exaggerated, and negative feedback from former employers has been left out. A resume is a sales pitch, not an objective report of the applicant's experience, character and skills. The applicant claims to have performed this task, but what actual evidence is there for that claim?

How can the prospective employer tell if an applicant is revealing his true character in a brief interview? We all know people can maintain a charming veneer that masks their real values, and that people will say whatever helps them get the job.

By accrediting your real-world projects in detail and providing verification from trustworthy sources, you will remove most of the risk from the hiring process.

Which applicant would you pick, all other qualifications being equal: the one with a resume full of unsupported claims and a few personal references of unknown trustworthiness, or the applicant with multiple projects detailing his skills and values and multiple sources that can be verified with basic online searches?

The first applicant is a high-risk hire, the second one is a low-risk hire because he's provided the prospective employer with a wealth of easily verifiable information about his skills, values and human and social capital.

We can summarize the process of accrediting yourself in five steps:

1. Learn and put into daily practice the eight essential skills/values of professionalism
2. Learn how to learn to mastery, that is, master new knowledge and apply new skills

3. Demonstrate your mastery and problem-solving by completing real-world projects
4. Assemble independently verifiable accounts of your abilities, experience, skills and professionalism from people with direct knowledge of your completed projects: colleagues, employers, supervisors, advisors, mentors, clients and peers.
5. Distribute your completed projects and third-party verifications to networks of people, agencies and enterprises that are active in your chosen field.

Each of these steps may be daunting to individuals accustomed to the factory model of assigned coursework and passively following instructions and also there is the added challenge that if you wanted to assemble independently verifiable accounts of your past projects these supervisors and colleagues may no longer be around because you don't work together anymore and he or she may feel they don't have time to respond to people they no longer work with. It is essential of acquiring the habit of learning new material and applying new skills to real-world problem-solving, to demonstrate perseverance and professionalism even in difficult circumstances, and to learn how to collaborate effectively with others. This is the process of building human and social capital.

Potential employers and clients have no way to verify your talents, abilities, experience, skills and values except what you provide them. The graduate who will be in demand is the one who demonstrates he/she possesses the eight essential skills and has real-world experience in creating value and perhaps even solving problems in a variety of settings.

The more people who know about your experience, skills and professionalism, the more likely it will be that someone will want to hire you or offer you an opportunity. Acquiring skills, demonstrating effectiveness, verifying one's abilities and professionalism and then distributing this information to appropriate networks—these are the essential steps to accrediting yourself.

Accrediting yourself doesn't just demonstrate your abilities to perform a specific task; being able to complete this multi-step process shows prospective employers and collaborators that you have everything it takes to help them accomplish their goals: grit, perseverance, integrity, good communication skills and professionalism. You will be demonstrating that you are the complete package, the real deal, the kind of person everyone wants to work with because you make working with you easy and make everyone you work with look good.

Let's examine these five steps in order.

The Process of Professionalism

One of the key characteristics of accrediting yourself is that it is a series of processes. Setting goals is important, but the real work is performed by establishing processes and habits that generate goal-oriented results: we are what we do every day.

For example, creativity isn't just the classic flash of genius: it is a process of consistent experimentation, testing the results and developing the idea or dropping it and moving on to the next one, a process.

Professionals are not born; they learn the values and acquire the habits of professionalism the same way we learn anything, with daily effort and practice directed goals. We covered this process in Section Three, Investing in Ourselves.

The goal of professionalism guides every step of our learning, job search, career development and how we deal with challenge, failure and disappointment.

One practical way to understand professionalism is to ask: how does a professional deal with unemployment? The answer is that the professional never considers himself unemployed; he is self-employed at all times, building human and social capital. The professional response to unemployment is to be productive for eight hours a day, regardless of the pay or lack thereof, day in and day out, rain or shine, because work isn't just about earning money, it's about creating value and meaning and living authentically.

This requires self-discipline and the development of productive habits, that is, investing in ourselves.

Let's review the eight essential skills of professionalism:

1. Learn challenging new material over one's entire productive life
2. Creatively apply newly-mastered knowledge and skills to a variety of fields
3. Be adaptable, responsible and accountable in all work environments
4. Apply a full spectrum of entrepreneurial skills to any task, that is, take ownership of one's work
5. Work collaboratively and effectively with others, both in person and remotely
6. Communicate clearly and effectively in all work environments
7. Continually build human and social capital, that is, knowledge and networks
8. Possess a practical working knowledge of financial records and project management

We've discussed various aspects of these skills in preceding sections, but now we will address key attributes of professionalism in greater depth. These include self-awareness and self-management, self- learning to mastery, maintaining motivation, building networks and becoming familiar with financial records and project management.

The key words in this section are learning and processes. Professionalism is lifelong learning and understanding that solving problems and creating value are the result of processes, not just ideas, inspiration, genius or goals. All of those play a part, but the work is done by processes. The higher we move up the value-creation/problem-solving chain, the more intuitive and flexible the processes tend to be. It's not so much what you know now; it's what you'll be learning today and tomorrow and applying to solving problems over the rest of your productive life.

Professionalism is valued in every field, white-collar and blue-collar, and in every person. Professionalism makes life and work easier, and problems easier to solve.

Self-Awareness/Self-Knowledge and Self-Management/Self-Discipline

The surest way to waste time and money and derail any project is to deal exclusively with unprofessional people: people who overpromise but under-deliver, who don't show up on time, make excuses for their lack of effectiveness, blame others for their own shortcomings, throw a tantrum when their work is critiqued, routinely make offensive remarks, exhibit disruptive behavior, dump unaddressed mental health issues on colleagues, inject personal issues into the workplace—the list is nearly endless but the results are always the same: unprofessional conduct is toxic to productivity and effectiveness. I worked in at a non-profit for four and a half years where I experienced the characteristics above first-hand and I was astounded at how managers continued to hire people with the above unprofessional characteristics over and over again. These demoralizing experiences lead me to devalue my place there.

I do not want to sound insensitive as we are all beset with a variety of inner conflicts, emotions, weaknesses and challenges; this is the human condition. But to solve problems, create value and collaborate effectively with others, we need to learn to separate our personal issues from getting the work done. This is the foundation of professional conduct and courtesy, and it requires a self-awareness/self-knowledge that guides our self-management and self-discipline.

Acquiring self-awareness and developing self-management are the first essential steps in becoming a professional. The process of accrediting yourself will open many opportunities to increase your self-awareness and practice self-discipline.

Why is self-knowledge so critical to success and personal happiness? There are two reasons: it takes self-knowledge to choose a career path that aligns with your interests and aptitudes and to reach the maturity—often called emotional intelligence—that defines professionalism. Professionalism requires a high level of maturity and self-awareness of our strengths and frailties.

Self-awareness is only the first half of developing empathy, maturity and emotional intelligence; the second half is developing the discipline needed to avoid self-destructive impulses and habits to get the better of us. The skills of self-management are needed to guide our growth as human beings and our professional pursuit of mastery.

One key aspect of self-awareness is the ability to put yourself in others' shoes, to see the situation from their perspective. This is essential to responding appropriately and professionally.

How does one develop self-management? Organize one's time and day as if you were self-employed, even if you're currently jobless; put yourself in the other person's shoes during every encounter, set professional standards for your conduct, habits, processes and responses, and set equally high goals for learning, productivity and effectiveness. Use both accomplishments and failures to add to your store of self-knowledge. Be equally forgiving of your own frailties and the frailties of others. Maintain a positive view of your chances to contribute to your own fulfillment and the effectiveness of other people, enterprises and groups in the pursuit of what interests you.

The process of accrediting yourself can help uncover interests and aptitudes, as completing real-world projects will reveal the depth of your interest in the work. If you find that completing the project has no appeal, this is evidence that there is a mismatch between the task and your personality and/or interests.

The ideal career is doing work that you pursue in your spare time because it's endlessly interesting. Accrediting yourself will help identify work that fits your personality type—for example, whether you prefer to work alone on detail-oriented tasks or whether you prefer to work in a dynamic environment of constant social interactions.

Career counseling can be helpful but there is no substitute for actually doing the work you think you may like. Completing real-world projects also gives you an opportunity to hone your professionalism and self-management skills.

In today's competitive economy, those whose interests and personalities align with their work will outperform those with little interest in the work other than the security of a paycheck. The accredit yourself process will help identify endeavors where you will be more successful and fulfilled than those that aren't a good match and where you are less likely to be competitive.

Clarifying What Money and Success Mean to You

One poorly understood and rarely mentioned aspect of self-knowledge is being aware of what money and success mean to you. This may seem obvious—we all want more money and greater success—but these beliefs are complex and have a great deal to do with our financial well-being and our day-to-day happiness.

Our beliefs about money are often hidden in subconscious patterns that affect our financial decisions in ways we don't fully understand. Thus someone might wonder why they're still financially insecure despite their high salary, and ignore their self-destructive spending habits that are obvious to everyone in their circle.

Pursuing definitions of success that are not really our own leads to frustration and unhappiness; how could somebody else's idea of success possibly be our own?

If we define success not just in terms of status, income or wealth but in our own fulfillment and day-to-day happiness, we have to explore what kind of work we actually enjoy doing every day. Knowing this will greatly improve the chances of success and fulfillment.

The Value of Authenticity in an Inauthentic World

I described the alienation of work and the substitution of intrinsically inauthentic consumerism for authentic meaning at the end of Section Two in Alienation and Work. One aspect of self-knowledge that is rarely discussed because it doesn't fit into the conventional view that increasing consumption increases happiness.

One pressing philosophical question that man has had throughout history is "what is the meaning of life"? Surely it cannot be to just buy more stuff. Consumerism is supposed to generate endless happiness, but what it actually generates is endless derangement and insecurity, as no amount of possessions, status, recognition or fame can turn the inauthentic into the authentic.

What can we do if conventional work and consumerism have little meaning?

We can start by being true to our authentic selves rather than pursuing someone else's dreams.

We can seek to own the means of production (our human and social capital) and the rewards of that production, eliminating the inherent alienation of performing interchangeable work for interchangeable companies and agencies.

If work generates little meaning in our lives, we can seek meaning outside of work in activities and networks that engage and nurture our best selves. For some people, this means spending time with their children, engaging in volunteer activities and pursuing creative endeavors. For others, it's gardening or building things of beauty and utility.

There are many definitions of authenticity; here are two points to authenticity:

1. What an individual owns lock, stock and barrel within themselves, that is, whatever is present that does not depend on outside acknowledgement.
2. Whatever an individual does when left to their own devices that gives them an innate sense of satisfaction that is not dependent on others' confirmation, and during which time passes quickly because the individual is absorbed in the activity.

From the time I was in college, then in my 30s and now in my early 40s I have pursued various career options such as a Master's degree, law school and finance. What I have discovered is that I really enjoy writing and developing webpages as well as other activities. In fact, I am a self-published author and this will be my second book.

A common bit of career advice is to pursue a high-paying, high-status job because the financial security will enable you to pursue the interests that give your life meaning.

I find this advice flawed on four counts.

1. In a rapidly changing economy, the promised financial security may be illusory. If a law degree leads to a job paying $40,000 a year rather than $170,000 a year, very little

security will have been gained, given the decades of student loan payments that typically accompany law school.
2. What if the cost of this security is daily misery? Was the cost worth the sacrifice? If happiness (that is, self-actualization) is the goal of life, then what sense does it make to sacrifice happiness for a financial security that supposedly enables the pursuit of happiness? Why not just pursue meaning and happiness right out of the gate?
3. Our culture is incapable of pricing the loss of authenticity, so the assumption that financial security is worth any sacrifice is unsupported.
4. Few that offer this advice disclose that the vast majority of high-status, high-salary jobs tend to be demanding and all-consuming, so there is precious little time or energy left to pursue anything else.

I do not mean to discount financial security. Some level of financial security makes life much easier than no financial security. The point here is that the ideal livelihood is one that enables and nurtures your authentic self, not one that sacrifices authenticity and happiness in a single-minded pursuit of financial security.

This is not an either/or choice; it is a balancing act. The goal is not unattainable perfection of authenticity, security and meaning; the goal is a set of skills that enable enough security, a way of life that enables enough opportunity to build human and social capital and work that provides enough meaning.

The Difference between Familiarity and Mastery

Familiarity with a field and mastery both create value and aid in solving problems. Having a working understanding of accounting and project management, for example, helps us make a realistic assessment of the overall situation and enables us to better organize resources. Mastery—thorough knowledge of a field and long practice in solving problems within it—generates a different premium.

We explained why this is so in Section Two: if the solution to a problem is not yet known, the work cannot be automated/commoditized. Work that is not tradable or reducible to processes that can be automated generates a premium.

Mastery—deep expertise based on experience and ownership of the work—is the key elements in value creation.

Mastery is not just a mix of knowledge, expertise and experience: it also requires ownership of the work, meaning that the master performs all work as if he owns every aspect of it: the process, the final product and the reputation that arises from the results of the work.

The worker who has knowledge and expertise but is incapable of owning their work can never achieve mastery.

It is vital that we understand that mastery is not just a collection of hard skills; it is also a value system of ownership of all work, no matter how menial or trivial it may appear to the outsider.

In traditional economies, mastery is gained by serving a long unpaid apprenticeship with a master craftsperson. The master often owns his/her own workshop, kitchen, lab, etc., and provides the apprentices with room and board. In exchange for years of hard labor, the master teaches the apprentices the processes and skills of the craft. Such apprentice-master craftsperson arrangements still exist in the traditional handcrafts of Japan.

How does one acquire mastery? There are three interconnected, reinforcing ways:

1. Self-learning, that is, when the student is the teacher
2. Help/instruction from a mentor/master of the trade
3. Practice, that is, completing real-world projects that solve problems or create value

Self-Learning to Mastery

We assume that everyone who attended school has learned how to learn, but this is not necessarily true. What we learned in school was how to learn by following instructions. The ability to teach ourselves, to self-learn to mastery, is a separate skill that we have to learn on our own.

In the classroom setting, the curriculum is structured so learning is accretive, that is, new learning builds on previous lessons. Self-learning must also be structured to be accretive.

Learning is not a smooth curve; it is inherently bumpy, and certain phases of the learning process may be so difficult that even motivated students may become discouraged. These are the critical points where outside resources such as mentors and peers can provide guidance and encouragement.

There are two basic methods that help the self-learning student over these rough spots:

1. Collaborate with peers pursuing the same goal
2. Develop mentor-apprentice relationships

Intense, focused study and concentrated work on problem-solving projects build knowledge and skills quickly: this is the equivalent of walking alone and walking fast.

But when the self-learner hits a wall, or needs encouragement, then developing mentors and peer collaborators enables learning over the long haul.

The first critical point where help from peers or mentors may be needed in the initial learning curve. Beginners may be discouraged by their lack of initial progress. Once they've gained the confidence provided by successfully completing the first step, they are better prepared to endure a learning curve in which rewards may be few and far between.

Some skills are inherently difficult and the initial learning curve is very steep, for example, learning to play a musical instrument such as a piano or learning to write software code.

Some skills are inherently difficult and the initial learning curve is very steep, for example, learning to play a musical instrument such as a piano or learning to write software code.

To advance requires self-discipline, time management and a number of other aspects of the eight essential skills. Without self-discipline and an accretive structure that builds on previous lessons, learning is piecemeal and cannot develop the ultimate skill of self-learning to mastery.

In the Asian tradition, the neophyte apprentice spends the first few years of apprenticeship doing low-skill, repetitive tasks to learn both self-discipline and the basics of the tradecraft. The objective is threefold:

1. To impress upon the student that the knowledge and skills being passed down to him are highly valued and cannot be gained easily;
2. To guide the student to the experience of mastery in the most basic skills of the trade; and
3. To instill self-discipline and the ability to persevere despite the rewards (empowerment, higher social standing, money) being slim to non-existent.

In other words, the objective is to teach the student that mastery of the trade can only be gained by rigorously following a structured series of accretive steps. Though it is tempting to think one can leapfrog from a few hastily-learned basics to near-mastery, this is the path to failure: each step in the trade must be mastered before it is possible to advance to the next. The master imposes this discipline not as punishment but as the necessarily rigorous path to mastery.

The authority of the mentor-master is not enforced by the government or an institution; rather, the authority flows solely from the mastery and the willingness to teach apprentices. These two traits are the source of the respect given to masters by their peers and apprentices.

This philosophy and program of learning is also the foundation of all martial arts instruction: there can be no mastery without rigorous adherence to strict rules of conduct and incessant practice of a highly structured series of accretive steps—deliberate, dedicated time spent focusing on improving one's skills. This is the core process of gaining mastery, and the ability to self-learn to mastery is a core skill needed to establish and earn a livelihood in today's economy.

Once the student has experienced learning as a process of accretive, structured steps that when pursued with self-discipline leads to the experience of mastery, he or she has gained the foundational skills of self-learning and the self-confidence to apply them to new fields.

Peers and mentors can help us along the way, but in an economy with few opportunities to establish traditional mentor-apprenticeship relationships, the self-learner must develop a network of peers and mentors who can help at critical junctures in the learning process.

These networks can help in three ways:

1. Provide solutions to problems that are blocking our progress.
2. Give us a motivational boost when we're discouraged.
3. Help us structure our learning plan to be accretive and result in mastery of the subject.

Resources for the Student as Teacher

Learning on one's own is often referred to as self-taught, but perhaps the more accurate description is the student as teacher. This term covers self-learning and students teaching each other. Books have always given us the means to learn on our own, but now online courses and tutorials have greatly expanded the tools of self-learning. The University of YouTube offers tutorials and short video lessons on everything from sewing on a button to electronics design.

Peer-to-peer collaborative learning is similarly untethered from the factory model of higher education; it can occur online or in a workshop or under a tree.

What is necessary is a structured course of study and an infrastructure that enables and encourages collaboration.

Careers in today's economy are increasingly an interconnected system of collaboration rather than a narrowly defined job within a hierarchy. Even within conventional careers, traditional areas of knowledge are spilling over and overlapping with previously distinct fields of expertise, requiring new levels of collaboration.

There are a number of different aspects to the student as teacher.

Collaboration occurs in two overlapping systems: in person and online. While we often collaborate with the same people in both areas, the two systems are not interchangeable and require slightly different skills and structures.

Peer-to-peer collaboration and teaching is now possible via digital media, for example online forums and tutorials, though this augments rather than replaces collaboration in real-world settings.

Technology has broadened the opportunities for the student to become the teacher via software-enabled adaptive learning. Anecdotally, developing-world students given appropriately programmed tablet computers can learn subjects on their own by playing preprogrammed educational games without any teacher at all.

In other words, in areas where teachers are unaffordable or scarce, cheap tablet computers and well-devised games and exercises provide learning for the cost of recharging the batteries.

Since the cost of reproducing and distributing digital lessons is essentially zero, an ever-widening spectrum of instructional videos offers each student a range of teaching approaches and methods which traverse the same material by different pathways.

A great many college-level open online courses are also available for free or for a modest fee. Individual students can review and then select the coursework and approach these online courses such as Udemy.com or the University of YouTube spheres for their learning style and aptitudes.

The challenge facing the student-as-teacher is to select a series of courses that lead to mastery.

The number of courses and tutorials is so large that it is daunting to design a series of courses aimed at a specific goal. This is where a mentor or more advanced peer can help by recommending a series of lessons or a pathway of tutorials that will take us to our goal of mastery.

Learning on our own is only one piece of achieving mastery (which is itself only one piece of accrediting yourself). There are two other pieces of mastery: assembling a network of collaboration, that is, a network of mentors and peers and finding real-world problems to solve that give us an opportunity to put our skills and knowledge into practice.

All three pieces work together. How do we find and recruit mentors and peers? We start with a specific field of endeavor/study and then find real-world problems to solve for groups, organizations and enterprises. The process of solving real problems for real organizations will aid the assembly of a network of collaboration which will then aid the selection of appropriate student-as-teacher coursework.

The process is not linear; it is an interactive model with feedback loops from each piece to every other piece. The choice of project/problem helps define the coursework/learning and the recruitment of mentors and peers.

Entrepreneurial Skills

If we had to summarize the eight essential skills, we might start with continuous learning and adaptability. We might also add entrepreneurial skills, but entrepreneurial is so over-used and poorly defined that the word requires some description to be meaningful.

Entrepreneurial skills in my definition mean:

1. Professionalism (that is, practicing the eight essential skills)
2. Owning your work
3. Being self-motivated

Entrepreneurism boils down to these three points; all other attributes are part of being professional, owning your work and being self-motivated.

Maintaining Motivation

One key component of self-learning is maintaining self-motivation and self-discipline.

The implicit assumption of conventional pedagogy is that students must be constantly motivated by teachers to learn. This reflects the inherent weaknesses of the factory model of education rather than human nature, as our minds are hard-wired to continuously refine our knowledge and skillsets.

The factory model doesn't lend itself to sustaining motivation; indeed, the assembly-line factory model pioneered by Henry Ford in the early 20th century was so unpopular with workers that many quit after a few days. The only motivator that improved the abysmal worker retention rate was significantly increasing the pay to overcome the workers' natural resistance to mind-numbingly boring hard labor.

We should not be surprised that the factory model of education has failed for many of the same reasons.

Studies of adults pursuing challenging long-term goals such as weight loss find that self-discipline and motivation is not enough, even within the cohort who graduated from college. Rather, these studies find collaboration and peer support is the one predictive factor in maintaining weight loss.

Assuming that students watching factory model courses at home can learn the eight essential skills, achieve mastery and apply these skills in the real world is a fatally flawed assumption. Real-world collaboration and mentor/peer support is an essential part of achieving mastery and accrediting yourself.

To nurture motivation, we first must understand its sources. There are a number of innate sources of motivation: our natural curiosity, for example, leads to learning. Learning practical skills is also inherently empowering, as acquiring new skills boosts our self-confidence and position in the economic hierarchy. This drive for self-betterment is a key source of motivation and self-discipline.

What motivates people to become their own teacher, that is, to be a self-directed learner? As a general rule, their motivation springs from a desire to learn how to do a specific task or solve a specific problem.

One basic way to maintain motivation is to design a series of accretive tasks or projects that are small enough to be manageable and that build on previous lessons and projects. Trying to tackle an enormous field of knowledge all at once is overwhelming, so breaking mastery into small steps is essential to maintaining motivation. Completing each small step is rewarding, even if progress on the entire project appears modest.

Willpower is also a key part of motivation. But willpower has a dual nature: on the one hand, it is a finite resource; we do not have unlimited reserves of willpower, so we must conserve it for the most critical tasks. One the other hand, willpower increases with practice: the more you exercise willpower, the more you have.

Willpower is like a muscle: overuse leads to exhaustion, but regular use leads to expanded capacity.

We covered using willpower to mold new productive habits in Section Three: Investing in Ourselves.

Setting goals is the third essential to maintaining motivation: without an overarching goal—achieving mastery and applying the eight essential skills—it's easy to lose our way and become distracted.

So maintaining motivation requires these four components:

1. Overarching goals that organize and prioritize our daily efforts (achieving mastery and the eight essential skills)
2. Investing our willpower to cement new habits that further our goals.
3. Breaking down every problem or project into its constituent parts, that is, bite-sized manageable steps that can be completed with available resources.
4. Collaborate with others, that is, establish a network of collaboration that supports our goals and efforts.

Collaboration is a two-way street: helping others also motivates us to stay engaged and to learn more so we can help others more.

Joining Networks of Collaboration

Recruiting mentors and peers who can help us learn new skills is a daunting task when starting from zero. We have a powerful ally in this, however: many people find it rewarding to help others.

People within a field, community or trade are already communicating and collaborating with each other in networks of collaboration; plugging into these existing networks is much easier than building your own from scratch—though sometimes that becomes necessary if the purpose of the network is new.

There are three core dynamics in networks of collaboration:

1. Reciprocity—giving as well as taking
2. It's the size of the network that matters, not the strength of each tie within it.
3. Networks of collaboration you join become part of your social capital

The key to building social capital is reciprocity—you're not just looking to get something, you're looking for a chance to contribute. Collaboration implies mutual benefit, the key to social capital.

The most productive networks are those that link to the broadest range of information, knowledge, and experience. Narrow expertise and limited circles of contacts severely limit problem-solving and thus the knowledge available to the network is limited. Interconnected circles of people joined on a voluntary basis include a much larger body of knowledge and expertise.

The most productive way to assemble a network of peers, mentors and collaborators is to join circles that are connected to other circles that have no connections to the ones you currently inhabit.

How do massively networked circles of people fuel innovation? They actively match problem-solvers to problems that need to be solved.

Networks of collaboration typically have a range of participants. Some might be specialists; others might not be very active while a few become super-users, the human equivalent of network routers that are linked to many more nodes than average users and who route more communication and information than less connected members. These are the most influential people in the network because they do the most. Networks of collaboration are informal and self-organizing doers, meaning that they are not hierarchical: super-users become influential by doing more.

The goal for new members of any network of collaboration is to identify the super-users with the most connections and the most influence. These are the people who will have heard of problems that need problem-solvers, for example, you. If you need help figuring out a difficult task, they will likely be able to recommend someone who is willing to help you.

Your first communication with a super-user should be to volunteer to help on projects that need participants. The more you do, the more you will learn and the greater your influence in the network. The most valuable people in any self-organizing network are: super-users, specialists who can solve particularly knotty or rare problems and go-to people, who can solve a variety of problems with minimal fuss and few resources. As a beginner, it will take time to become a super-user, and you may not yet have high-level skills that make you a specialist. But virtually anyone with the eight skills of professionalism can become a go-to person.

Everyone loves go-to people because they solve problems without making a financially or emotionally costly production of the task. They take ownership of the task and locate and organize the people and resources to do so. They might ask super-users for suggestions, but they figure out what's needed and organize the people and processes.

Our task then is to find ways to plug into existing networks of people who are studying or working in our field of interest. There are many ways to do so: for example, taking a local community college class and seeking projects to collaborate on with other students.

Joining a community group is another way to start making connections to wider circles.

The most dynamic parts of the economy—start-ups, co-ops, and other parts of the community economy—are opt-in (that is, participants freely join, participate and leave) doers, where those who contribute the most tend to accumulate the most influence. Your social capital will expand as you accomplish more in doer type of organizations, as those within these organizations know you are directly responsible for solving problems and creating value.

Your efforts to help someone you don't yet know personally will form weak ties to that person and the circles he/she inhabits, and these weak ties will add innovative problem-solving power to your own network. Aiding others whenever possible is an investment in the power of weak ties to build your own social capital. Not every investment pays off, the cumulative effect of mentoring and helping others is profound.

Social-media networks are not substitutes for active participation for doers and organizations where your engagement makes a difference—and others know that you've made a difference.

Actively Seek Problems to Solve

The starting point of accrediting yourself is finding a real-world problem to solve that demonstrates your abilities and skills. Let's start by comparing this process to the conventional job search.

The process of finding problems to solve introduces you to people who may become trusted mentors or peers.

The benefit of volunteering in a community organization is that the people who devote time and energy to such organizations (churches, environmental issues, local sports, etc.) are self-selected doers who generally know many people, some of whom might be able to help you as peers or mentors—the power of weak ties.

The community economy tends to be composed of doers in which those who contribute the most have the most influence. This is an excellent environment for anyone seeking to make a difference (that is, solve problems and create value) and make connections to people who might become collaborators, peers and mentors, as doers tend to collaborate with other doers.

Contrast this with the conventional approach, where the student gets a college degree, prepares a resume detailing their coursework and work history and then applies for a series of jobs. The degree and resume are presumed to accredit the graduate's knowledge, skills and readiness to create value for an employer. The employer reviews numerous resumes and interviews graduates, and then selects the one with the most impressive resume and academic performance.

The flaws in this process are readily apparent. A degree and a resume offer minimal evidence of the graduate's soft skills, ability to solve problems, learn on his own and create value. Resumes are seen as a branch of public relations, crafted to place the applicant in the best possible light and pass through all the conventional human resources department filters.

The process is passive: the graduate plays a numbers game based on probabilities, that is, if I send out 100 resumes I will get five interviews and if I get five interviews I will get one job offer.

But experience suggests this probabilities-based approach no longer works: many graduates have sent out hundreds of resumes and applications and not received a single response, much less a job offer.

This conventional process is miles away from the practical approach of directly accrediting your knowledge, skills, values and problem-solving abilities within networks of collaboration.

Graduates face a chicken-egg problem: employers want work experience, but how do you get experience if no one will hire you due to lack of experience? The answer is to go out in the real world and seek problems to solve within organizations and enterprises.

This is not as difficult as it may appear at first glance. Let's start with the basic sectors of the economy: the state (government), private enterprise and the community economy, my terms for every organization and activity that is neither funded by the state nor organized around the goal of making a profit. This includes churches (by which I mean all houses of worship) and a wide spectrum of community groups.

Each sector has formal positions that are difficult to obtain. But each sector has less formal parts where volunteers can make a difference. In government, this includes city agencies; in private enterprise, this includes many small businesses and start-ups, and in the community economy, this includes a wide spectrum of local groups and organizations.

A great many community groups and organizations lack proper accounting and public relations programs, due to limited staffing, funding and expertise. Finding a problem to solve that fits your interests and field of endeavor may be as easy as walking into local churches, environmental organizations, neighborhood groups, volunteer-based sports programs or any one of hundreds of other community-economy organizations and asking what projects need doing or problems that need solving.

The list is generally long enough and varied enough that the willing volunteer can find something that aligns with their field of interest and goals of mastery. Data entry, bookkeeping, and public relations (social media, outreach to members, contacting local media, etc.) are often unmet needs/problems that need to be solved.

Completing these projects (or organizing a system that will outlast your own participation) creates value for the organization. This is what employers hire people to do: solve problems and create value. This is the goal of offering one's services—not just to donate time but to identify serious problems that you can solve and document to accredit your abilities and experience.

Starting this search for problems to solve/value to create while you are enrolled in a class is ideal, as people are naturally inclined to help students and to view them as a potential resource. If you want to get into financial services, for example, if you contact small investment management firms asking for work you will likely be told there are no openings. If you contact these same firms as a student asking for some guidance from an established expert in the field, you will likely be invited to meet with the owner or key staff.

In the meeting, your inquiries should focus on identifying the key problems of the business—problems that limit expansion, profitability, retention of clients, etc. People might hesitate to speak openly about such problems with job applicants, but they are more likely to be honest with a student who is seeking to understand the business as part of a research project.

If you are out of school, then launch an independent study project that serves the same goal. If you're interested in investment management, start managing an imaginary portfolio as if it were real client money. Learn everything you can about portfolio management, risk management, etc.—the constituent parts of investment management—and then share your conclusions with small investment management firms and ask for feedback.

Whatever field of endeavor you have chosen to master, reach out to enterprises, groups and organizations that might benefit from your interest and desire to solve their most pressing problems.

Contacting a variety of community groups and small enterprises will give you a feel for the range of problems that organizations need solved and also introduce unexpected connections and pathways to your goal of mastery and self-accreditation.

For example, someone who wants to gain construction/building skills might naturally start by contacting builders and contractors. But more than likely they will encounter the same difficulties mentioned above—a lack of credentials and experience. A more likely way to gain experience might be to ask local churches if you can help with any building maintenance projects, since virtually every older building has maintenance issues that require a range of construction skills. Whoever is handling the maintenance will likely welcome a motivated volunteer, and the person will likely offer connections to others in the field.

Newsletters need to be written and distributed, grant proposals written and pitched, mailing lists culled and updated, subcommittees formed—all of which can certify your abilities, leadership and professionalism in a variety of other fields and jobs.

Innovation and problem-solving often depend not just on narrow expertise but on networks, cross-pollination of disciplines and a variety of experiences.

Learn to use the networks that already exist in organizations to help solve problems, and use the power of weak ties to deepen your social capital.

This process of helping a community group, city program or enterprise solve critical problems naturally introduces you to key participants and contributors in those organizations. Once these people see that you actually complete projects that create value and are able to collaborate effectively with others, they will naturally be disposed to offer you whatever help they can in widening your network of peers, mentors, potential employers or people who might introduce you to potential employers.

Tackling problems or projects for an organization does three things simultaneously. It directs your course of learning as you seek the knowledge, skills and contacts needed to solve the problem, it gives you real-world experience in problem-solving and collaborating with others, and it introduces you to a widening circle of people who will help you assemble a network of collaboration, that is, a network of knowledgeable peers and mentors who can accredit your knowledge, accomplishments, values and skills.

It's important to remember that though others can assist you or offer guidance, real learning only comes from what you do yourself.

Documenting and Sharing Your Completed Projects

The documentation phase of accrediting yourself is a four-step process:

1. Document the project you contributed to or completed as if you were a reporter, with a synopsis or summary, quotes from participants, photos and a brief description
2. Recruit others you worked with to verify your role
3. Post this documentation online where others can easily access it
4. Distribute the site to your collaborations and appropriate networks within your field of interest

Remember to put yourself in the shoes of a prospective employer or client; they want a description of what problems arose and how they were resolved.

Remember that the real work is done not by setting goals but by establishing and perfecting cost-effective, productive processes. Don't just document the steps you took (updating mailing lists, switched the newsletter to a more attractive template, etc.); document the process of collaboration ("After meeting with the executive director and the outreach committee, I drew up a proposal to make the newsletter a tool to recruit new members and not just report on activities"), how you assessed what wasn't working well/needed to be fixed and your proposed systemic solution.

In other words, the solution wasn't just a one-time updating of the group's mailing list; your solution was to make a well-thought out collaborative assessment of the entire process of producing and distributing the newsletter, and asking if the newsletter was truly serving the core needs of the group.

This process culminated in your proposed systemic solution, that is, a clearly documented process that someone after you could follow to produce the newsletter without having to reinvent the wheel.

Various obstacles invariably arise in the course of any project, and how you overcome obstacles, objections, conflicts, errors, etc. will be of keen interest to prospective employers and clients, as this documents your problem-solving and professional abilities.

Remember that this documentation is evidence of your ability to communicate clearly and succinctly. Keep it simple, well-organized: who, what, when, where, what problems arose, how they were solved, how the organization/client gained from the completed project.

The process of documenting your contributions may proceed slowly or haltingly, but the value accumulates with each project. Your first project may not look overly impressive, but ten such projects will reflect all the qualities employers, collaborators and clients value: professionalism, perseverance, leadership, ability to learn on your own, problem-solving, value creation, communication, and ability to collaborate effectively with others.

Soliciting Third-Party Verification and Testimonials

The advantage of the new media today is that we no longer are at the mercy of a critic employed by the newspapers and magazines to offer review of films, books, restaurants, art exhibits, etc. Now we can rely on the crowd-sourced consensus of dozens or hundreds of other users/customers. While one individual may have an axe to grind or a bias that slants their perception of a film, café, etc., the motivations of hundreds of users are filtered out simply by the lack of material gain or influence any one reviewer can accrue.

The importance of these reviews is that those who are only seeking to game the system rarely bother to laboriously assemble a meaningful portfolio of reviews first.

If you accomplished goals, finished projects, solved problems and added value, a simple reporting of the facts is testimony of your values, skills and abilities.

The ideal set of testimonials is provided by people you worked with closely whose own value in various networks is easily verified online.

The more ties a person has that can be quickly verified as legitimate, the more value their testimonials will have.

If key people are too busy to write a few paragraphs verifying your completed project (as will often be the case—it's nothing personal, it's just that they're over-committed and over-scheduled), write a brief, clearly written report yourself (who, what, when, where, how and the goal accomplished) and ask them to sign it or attach their name to it.

If you can't get testimonials from well-connected professionals, then get honest reports from as wide a variety of colleagues and collaborators as possible.

Your blog/website should not be a static project that is completed and abandoned; it should constantly be revised, updated and improved to reflect your own advancement.

The Value of a Professional Blog/Website

Many people rely on social media such as Twitter or Facebook to present their public selves, but these formats do not lend themselves to serious, well-organized and professionally presented documentation. Only a website or blog that you completely own and manage can document your professional skills and completed projects.

As with every other aspect of accredit yourself, creating a website to present yourself and your work offers a valuable opportunity to display your communication and design skills. You want your website to send the message of being "professional and productive" and you can do that by developing a cleanly organized, clearly composed website.

The templates and tools needed to build a simply but professional blog or website are free, and tutorials on how to do so abound. Templates are a starting point, but the first thing anyone looking at your blog/website will notice is whether you have the skills to go beyond simple template and customize your site to optimally communicate your projects and skillsets.

Your blog or website will have a unique URL (web address) that will enter the collaborative networks you have joined or are developing. Since social media and web-based communication is now core to every enterprise and organization, displaying your working knowledge of web-based media is an important step in accrediting your ability to communicate clearly.

Accreditation and Self-Employment

The process of accrediting your value to prospective employers and accrediting your value to prospective clients is identical. This is how many people become self-employed: someone sees their excellent work and asks them to do the same work for them. Though many people view self-employment as insecure and more responsibility than they care to shoulder, from the point of view of the changing economy, everyone is self-employed: those working for others are simply temporarily lending their self-employment skills to others.

The ideal collaborator is someone who sees no line between employment and self-employment, someone who owns their work regardless of the circumstance. They operate with the same values and ownership whether they are employed by an organization, collaborating with others on a project or are self-employed. This is the ultimate adaptability and thus the ultimate security.

The Goal of Accrediting Yourself: To Be the Only One Who Does What You Do

If we had to summarize the goal in accrediting yourself, start by emphasizing the verification of our adaptability, ability to self-learn, professionalism and entrepreneurial skills.

But perhaps the ultimate goal of accrediting yourself is to be the only one who does what you do.

This is a succinct, profound encapsulation of creating value, the matrix of work and the premium of labor: you do not want to demonstrate that you are one of the best in a field; you want to stake out a piece of the emerging economy that is yours alone.

This does not necessarily require an astounding level of accomplishment; it also characterizes a person with a set of experiences and skills that cross-pollinate in unique ways to create value and solve new problems.

Section Six: Putting It All Together

Let's put everything we've learned together in a few final points.

What Is Security?

It is human nature to seek both security and novelty, and on first glance these may appear to be mutually exclusive: security means safe, stable and known, while novelty means change and exposure to the unknown/new.

In state-cartel capitalism, there are three recognized sources of financial security:

1. Gain access to the spoils system of entrenched elites (such as Wall Street) via family connections or connections gained through elite universities or other elitist portals
2. Get hired by sprawling bureaucracies (typically government agencies or government contractors) that are designed to dissipate accountability so that no one can be fired for underperformance, laziness or incompetence

3. Launch a business that either generates substantial, stable profits or that has new technology that can be sold to a large corporation for an immense gain

In general, the number of openings in the spoils system of entrenched elites is very limited. Roughly 15% of the workforce (22 million people) work for government at all levels, and millions more work for government contractors that are basically agencies of the state. But since those who value this type of security have self-selected to work for government agencies precisely to obtain this security, the number of openings is largely limited to replacement of retirees.

While many dream of starting a hyper-successful business, relatively few have the financial, human and social capital needed to start and grow such an enterprise.

So what do the rest of us do for security?

Let's start by reviewing what we learned about capitalism and the emerging economy. We found that entrenched elites and bureaucracies are self-liquidating, meaning that they are organized to respond to diminishing returns by doing more of what has failed spectacularly, that is, precisely what created the diminishing returns in the first place.

This is why I describe our financial system as dysfunctional and predatory. It is a system in decline as it has consumed all the available oxygen and has no more room for further expansion.

The same can be said of all the other cartels: pharmaceuticals, national defense, healthcare, higher education, etc.: every cartel has already consumed all the oxygen available in its space and is far down the road of diminishing returns. Every dominant cartel in the system is at the top of the S-Curve, poised for an unexpected and uncontrolled decline.

The more sclerotic, hidebound, inefficient and wasteful the cartel or bureaucracy, the more vulnerable it is to creative destruction. The gains will be as outsized as the inefficiencies destroyed.

In other words, the large-scale bureaucracies that appear secure in the mid-2014 are less secure than is generally believed.

Jobs characterized by day-to-day insecurity such as driving a taxi, doing nails, braiding hair, or any sort of free-lance project-based collaboration is actually more secure than supposedly secure jobs that come with all sorts of hidden fragilities and systemic dependencies.

This book is to prepare the "do-ers" so that they will receive the rewards that come with applying adaptability, professionalism and entrepreneurial skills. The cost of this security is day-to-day volatility, dissent and variation, all of which provide the critical information needed to maintain the system's adaptability and vigor.

What I am saying here is that this so-called stability found in bureaucratic government jobs and non-profit organizations that receive public funding breed failure.

Embracing the security of bureaucracies and entrenched-interests is actually a bet that creative destruction will magically cease destroying what is inefficient and unproductive, that diminishing returns can continue until the output is less than zero and that bureaucracies and cartels will all magically escape the S-curve.

Embracing what we're told is insecure—self-employment, project-based collaboration, worker-owned cooperatives, and so on—is actually more secure in a rapidly changing economy.

New Models of Ownership, Work and Collaboration

Any cartelization of an industry is ripe for creative destruction. These large-scale state agencies and corporate cartels appear to be stable and impervious to change, much less creative destruction. But these extremes of ownership and control mean the opportunities for new, more productive arrangements are as unlimited as the market. But since these new markets and arrangements are not yet well-known, the vast majority of people are unaware of them.

As we have discussed at length, human and social capital are the means of production, and the tools for producing goods and services are falling rapidly in cost, meaning that they are within the grasp of far more people than ever before.

Since doing interchangeable work for interchangeable bureaucracies is intrinsically alienating, and not owning your work or the output of your work is also alienating, the innate human desire for authenticity and fulfillment means those arrangements which reduce alienation will attract the energy and capital of those who cannot bear to sacrifice themselves for an illusory security.

There are a number of new models for ownership, work and collaboration: worker-owned cooperatives, consumer-owned cooperatives, community-owned resources open to participation by a resident, project-based collaborative arrangements and self-organizing networks that replace hierarchical bureaucracies. The access-based model (as opposed to the ownership model) is also creating opportunities to do more with less. The no-middleman model is another alternative that reduces costs and opens new distribution opportunities from producer to end consumer.

The intelligence and creativity of the opt-in network exceeds that of a centralized hierarchical bureaucracy. Doers are inherently more transparent, adaptable, accessible and democratic than centralized hierarchies.

The other key feature of such alternatives is the workers/participants own the work and the output. Work that is alienating when performed for the state or corporation becomes authentic and purposeful when those producing the work own the processes and the output.

The 40-hour a week job working for a single employer is another model that is no longer adaptable enough to fit new arrangements of collaboration. The job of the future is a hybrid work model. Hybrid work draws purpose and meaning from a variety of projects and work, some paid, some unpaid, some compensated by value other than money; hybrid work generates a mix of income from a variety of sources and investments in yourself.

Hybrid work offers several income streams, perhaps mixing self-employment with multiple sources of paid work. The key features of hybrid work are adaptability, flexibility, ownership of work choices, some self-employment/collaborative work and some income from investing in yourself and your own enterprises.

Opportunities are most abundant in sectors not under the control of the centralized state or cartel-corporations: the doers in the community economy which is focused on sustainability and doing more with less.

Integrating the Matrix of Work

Let's integrate what we learned about the matrix of work and the premium generated by labor with what we've learned about accrediting yourself: focus on developing a spectrum of skills that includes utilizing new networks and technologies. Seek skills that create hybrid vigor, that is, skills that can be cross-pollinated to solve new problems. Focus on accrediting these high-value, commoditization-resistant skills.

If you need to develop skills that can generate income right away, focus on acquiring skills that can be learned to mastery in a few months. Once you've reached that plateau, you'll be able to fund the longer-term learning you will need to gain mastery of skills that take years to develop.

From the perspective of the matrix of work, security can be defined as owning a variety of skills, and/or specialized skills that are immune to commoditization. Those with a variety of skills will always be able to create value in some capacity.

Moving to an Infrastructure of Opportunity

Even the most talented, skilled individual will be unable to create value or solve problems if there is no opportunity for his/her skills. Even the hardiest seed cannot grow if it lands on desert hardpan.

This means you may have to move to a place that offers opportunity or assemble an infrastructure of opportunity with like-minded people. Assembling the infrastructure from scratch is difficult and time-consuming and in my experience I don't believe that an infrastructure of opportunity exists in all urban zones.

Managing Change

Famed psychiatrist Carl Jung proposed that humans use four principal psychological functions to process experience: sensation, intuition, feeling, and thinking. The Myers-Briggs personality test seeks to divide those who predominantly rely on one or two of the functions into various personality types.

In other words, certain personality types may be more deeply impacted by an intellectual insight than others. For example, some people may be predisposed to read about the role of fitness in health and start a fitness program based solely on that knowledge, while others have to experience a heart attack before changing their daily lifestyle habits.

While insight, knowledge and direct experience are all important motivational starting points, the key to transformation is to design a process that brings about the change we want. For example, if we want to improve our health and fitness, we must first design a process that yields the changes we want: an exercise routine and a diet that we can live within the long-term. A process that doesn't fit our personality is likely to fail: if a person is not a morning person, a plan that requires awakening at 5a.m. for a job in darkness is not sustainable.

In a similar way, a creative solution to a problem might suddenly occur to us, but the implementation of that solution typically requires a process.

In everyday life, processes are habits: the process of improving fitness results from fitness routines becoming habits.

We resist change for all sorts of reasons, starting with our innate preference to conserve whatever has worked in the past as trying something new entails risk: the change might yield no gain at all.

But we may also resist making productive changes because the motivators don't activate our personality type. We may want to change but lack the ability to develop a process that yields the desired output (a new habit, a new routine, etc.).

Fortunately, we can learn how to develop processes by studying project management and systems: what process will yield the results we want?

Each of us has a comfort zone of creativity and routines. Studies suggest that pushing ourselves outside of our comfort zones yields new insights. We also know that advances occur when concepts and ideas from one field cross-pollinate knowledge in different fields.

Managing change is easier if we have self-knowledge about our personality type and if we develop processes that will get us where we want to be, including pushing ourselves out of our comfort zones and developing a wide based of cross-pollinating knowledge that generates new insights and values.

Become the Person Everyone Who Owns the Output Wants to Work With

What kind of person do we want to work with? For most of us, it's someone who is honest, generous, good-natured, forgiving and competent, someone who is a good listener and who communicates clearly, and someone who keeps their own personal troubles out of the workplace.

But if you ask those who own the output of the work, for example, everyone in a worker-owned cooperative, the demands are even higher. When the output is everyone's livelihood, what people want is professional ownership of the work and dedication to customers, clients and the quality of the product. They want colleagues with entrepreneurial skills who get the job done with a minimum of waste. They want people who know how to learn new processes and material efficiently. They want people who can maintain a sense of humor even under stress, people who can maintain a focus on priorities that serve the interests of the group, not just themselves. They want people who ask more of themselves than they ask of anyone else. They want people who can accept honest criticism as a gift rather than an insult. They want people who are able to praise others when praise is due. They want people who seek mastery for the fulfillment and meaning mastery provides.

They want professionalism, because professionals get more done in less time and with less waste than non-professionals.

Anyone who can become the person everyone who owns the output wants to work with will find work once they join the appropriate network of collaboration and accredit themselves.

For those who can do this, success becomes inevitable.

Luis Daniel Cortes

Philadelphia, Pennsylvania

October 2014

www.ingramcontent.com/pod-product-compliance
Lightning Source LLC
Chambersburg PA
CBHW051705170526
45167CB00002B/546